Leonie Charlton lives in Glen Lonan, Argyll. She writes poetry, fiction and creative non-fiction and is a graduate of the MLitt in Creative Writing at University of Stirling. Her work is informed by a deep attachment to the West Coast of Scotland where she spends most of her time. She enjoys walking and time with horses as ways to feel her way into landscape, to explore whatever reveals itself through quiet attentive travel. She also loves to sleep on the hill, to experience, over and over again, the privilege of re-entering that world when she wakes.

www.leoniecharlton.co.uk

MARRAM

Memories of Sea and Spider Silk

LEONIE CHARLTON

SANDSTONE PRESS

First published in Great Britain in 2020
Sandstone Press Ltd
Suite 1, Willow House
Stoneyfield Business Park
Inverness
IV2 7PA
Scotland

www.sandstonepress.com

Sandstone Press is committed to a sustainable future. This book is
made from Forest Stewardship Council ® certified paper.

ISBN: 978-1-913207-10-6
ISBNe: 978-1-913207-11-3

Cover design by Two Associates
Typography by Iolaire, Newtonmore
Printed and bound by CPI Group (UK) Ltd, Croydon, CR0 4YY

For my mother, Kathryn Ade,
for her inimitable joie de vivre.

Acknowledgements

So many people supported me on this journey through the Outer Isles. Too many to mention here, but I extend my heartfelt thanks to them all, to those who helped us during our travels with their warmth and hospitality and advice, to those who so generously shared their stories. Lasting gratitude to my three companions on the trip: Shuna Shaw, her wise, good-humoured and treasured company – we have travelled many paths together and I look forward to many more; the Highland ponies, Ross and Chief, who have taught me, and brought me, so much – their hearts are vast, their level of presence endlessly inspiring. Thanks also to writer and activist Alastair McIntosh whose book *Poacher's Pilgrimage* broadened my vision and enriched my experience.

Deepest thanks to my husband Martin without whom this journey wouldn't have been possible, his generosity and unstinting support constantly amaze me – thank you from the furthest reaches of my heart. Thanks also to our three children, Brèagha, Finn and Oran, who put up with my absences, both while away, and then at home when I don't answer questions, burn the dinner, am utterly lost to my internal worlds; their patience means the world to me.

On my writing journey I would like to thank in particular the Creative Writing Department at University of Stirling, to the tutors Liam Bell, Meaghan Delahunt, Chris Powici and Kathleen Jamie, who opened up new worlds of words to me, ones founded on integrity and possibility. Sophy Dale for her support during the writing of the first draft of *Marram*, I honestly don't know if it would ever have happened without her help with time management and her generous encouragement. Frances Ainslie for her writerly sisterhood and eagle-sharp editing eye. To *Island Review* who published an extract from an earlier version of this book. Finally, thanks to Robert Davidson and the whole Sandstone Press team.

Author's Note

I inherited a love of wildlife and landscape from my parents. My feeling of interconnectedness with the natural world defines and sustains my existence. Throughout this book I have taken the poetic licence of capitalising plant and animal names; not on every occasion, but in the moments that call for particular emphasis on a plant or animal's presence. It feels crucial, in these times of climate crisis and mass species extinction, that we bring our full awareness and appreciation to the diversity around us. I have been inspired by writers such as Glennie Kindred who capitalises all tree names in her book *Walking with Trees*, and Robin Wall Kimmerer, who in *Braiding Sweetgrass* breaks with grammatical convention to write freely of Maple and Heron.

Leonie Charlton
Taynuilt, Argyll
2020

Contents

Preface

I'm sitting in my writing box in Glen Lonan, Argyll. It's early September, and three months since I got back from riding through the Outer Hebrides with my friend Shuna and our two Highland ponies, Ross and Chief. I can see Ross now, grazing on grass that has lost its summer sheen. The forested hillside rises up behind him, a single Rowan in full bright-berry stands out amongst the Birch and Oak. Beyond the soft shrug of these trees, half hidden in cloud, is Ben Cruachan. The writing box is the back of a refrigerated van that my father converted. He took out the steel meat hooks, put in windows and a door. Despite his attention to detail it relies on a dehumidifier to stay dry. Today is my first time in here for a while and I'm aware of its particular smell; a combination of damp emulsion and plywood, metal and mould. I push the window open wide and breathe in the cuspy autumn air.

Bracken has grown up past the windowsill. Coppery tones seep upwards from the ground and colour the under-fronds. There are Thistles too – purple flowers long gone but the heads are still holding onto tufts of down, silver turned to peaks of grey after weeks of rain. A single Foxglove folds across, its leaves riddled with rust-edged holes, empty flower cups darkening to

xiii

a loam brown. On the inside of the windowsill is a stem of Marram Grass I found in my saddlebags after the trip. It is sharp and lucent. It reminds me of how I'd felt coming home, bright and still after all those slow-spent hours in the marram and cotton grass.

My mother passed to me a passion for horses which has been a lifeline, a source of love and grounding throughout my life. My relationship with her was fraught with pain and misunderstanding, at times I'd wondered if life would be better without her. Then she died and I was broken. Almost seven years after her death, long enough for nearly every cell in my body to have renewed itself, it felt like the grief and regret were intensifying. I was bone-weary of the guilt, *a redundant emotion* Mum herself had always said. She'd been a jeweller and a passionate collector of beads. During the months of planning for the Hebrides trip an idea had formed to leave a trail of beads for Mum. Where better than through this archipelago that she'd loved, itself a necklace of granite and sand, schist and gneiss, strung on streams of salt and fresh water.

I have loved the Hebrides for decades, ever since travelling to some of the islands on work-trips with my father, Max Bonniwell, who was a vet in Oban. One summer Dad took my younger brother and me on a camping trip through the Outer Hebrides, memories of that fortnight remain amongst the most luminous of my life. I associated the islands with him and everything he embodied, which was the opposite of the emotional, cultural and physical chaos of life with Mum. Dad represented safety and stability. He smelt of veterinary disinfectant. He knew the names of all the seabirds and of all the sailing boats. Mum had also travelled widely in the Hebrides, but I'd never been out there with her, and now, in this unexpected way, was my chance.

The islands and strands we crossed, the people and wildlife

we met, the days of travel alongside the ponies, the memories that surfaced as I laid down beads, would all wrest changes in my inner landscape. At the head of Loch Rèasort, where Harris meets Lewis, I would nearly lose my pony. I would be stripped back by fear in that place and find my own bedrock that had been hidden under layers of life-silt. The journey would prove to be a pilgrimage of love and personal sea-change. *Marram* is the story of how I found new relationships with my mother and with myself. It is also a love story of place, not just of how environment renews and nourishes us human beings, but also of how our wakefulness, our attentiveness, may give something back in return. We leave behind footprints steeped in appreciation, and perhaps the best gift of all to the sand and peat, two sets of smooth hoof prints.

Today seems a fitting day to start writing about this journey. The apples are half turned to red on the trees outside. A young Buzzard is mewing, he has been doing it for weeks while he flies elliptical circles. Each day the calls are getting stronger and higher. He is on his own now.

Day 1 to Day 14: Castlebay to Leverburgh

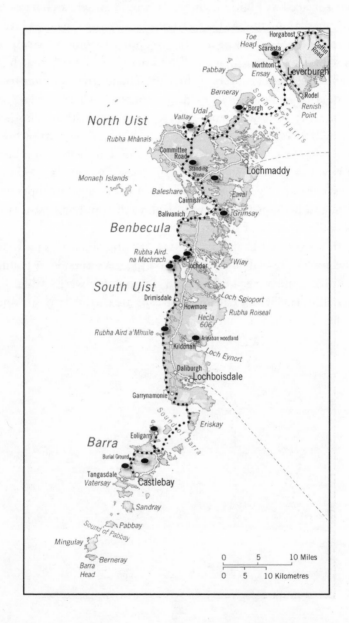

Day 15 to Day 22: Leverburgh to Callanish

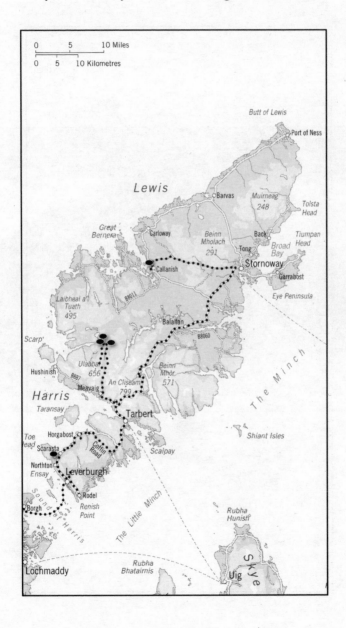

DAY ONE

Oban to Barra

Our stuff was spread out across the metal-rimmed table in the dining area of MV Isle of Lewis: water bottles, camera cases, lip salve, cable ties, bananas, a stack of pink OS maps numbered 31, 22, 18, 14 and 8. There were two books placed face down at significant pages: Pocket Walking Guide No 3, Western Isles; The Outer Hebrides, 40 Coast and Country Walks. A purse full of Mum's beads was there too.

We moved everything to one side when the smiling steward brought across our plates of fish and chips and rolling peas. 'So, here's to our trip then,' said Shuna, her eyes aquamarine in the sunlight coming through the salt-chalked glass. We clinked the tops of our Peroni beer bottles. Shuna and I had been friends for fifteen years and we'd done several long horse trips together. We were both aware there were big gaps in our planning this time, but there wasn't much we could do now, just hope that everything would work out. I told her about the man talking on the radio that week of the benefits of travelling without plans, how it leaves you open to new experiences, to meeting people in a different way. I'd taken it as a positive sign.

We drank quickly and, sitting there, watching diving Gannets spill the sea into spindrifts of white, our shoulders began to soften. The water bottles rolled backwards and forwards across the table as the sea pushed the boat up beneath us. I picked up the bead purse. It wasn't exactly classy, made of soft plastic, the words 'LAS VEGAS' repeated in gold and silver and white across a shiny black background. Mum definitely wouldn't have approved, but it was the perfect size and had a good sturdy zip. I opened it and looked inside at the huddle of beads, wondering where they would all end up. There was also a little roll of ivory silk thread which I'd found in Mum's bead drawers. I'd originally thought I'd take a fishing line to tie the beads onto things because it was tough and wouldn't weather. Then I'd started to worry that a bird might get caught in it, or worse. The silk thread would decompose eventually, but there was no need for the beads to stay put forever; Mum's necklace would be fluid, made up of gestures of emotion in a certain place, in a certain moment. It would change shape, the beads free to move through storms and tides and seasons.

The boat rolled again and I felt my guts tilt. I tried to close the zip but a loose strand of silk had snagged in the zipper. I carefully teased it out, my fingers touching this spool of thread that Mum must have handled countless times. I thought of her hands and felt that old familiar wash of pain. I could see her fingers now, red from the cold. They were always cold. We were all always cold, living in those old stone-walled houses and barely able to afford to keep one room warm. She used to say that her hands were ugly, that they were manly. She didn't wear rings because she hadn't wanted to draw attention to her hands. I remember watching them for hours while she worked, her dexterity, her skill, even after the first brain tumour when they trembled and trembled. Yet still she'd persevere with threading the tiniest crystals, the tiniest seed pearls, taking as long as it took. Handling things she loved in those hands she didn't love. Holding treasures between her fingertips, angling them to the light.

My brothers, Will and Tom, and I always said that she should have been rich; she had a taste for expensive things, for luxury, and yet had so little of that in her life. I knew she wouldn't have approved of all the beads I'd chosen. I'd been in a hurry that day. Had found it difficult opening those drawers that still smelt of her. I'd kept thinking about her nails, always filed smooth so they wouldn't snag on the thread. Then in her last few years how they had been bright red. How she'd had acrylic nails 'done' by a professional every month. Standout nails. So, did that mean she'd made peace with her hands by then? I hadn't asked, that would have felt dangerously like connection. I was sorry that we hadn't got a professional in to do her nails when she was in the Lynne of Lorne Nursing Home, that we'd let somebody we never met do them, a volunteer. Yes, her hands. They haunted me. Even when she was dying, and the rest of her rattled tiny, her hands had stayed big. Right to the end. I looked at my own hands as I pulled the zip closed. I didn't know whose hands I had, but I knew they weren't my mother's.

It was bright out on deck. The bolted-down plastic seats were coral red under the overhead sun. The ferry's jade-streaked wake trailed back down the Sound of Mull towards the mainland. I could make out the double peak of Ben Cruachan, my home hill. We'd already passed the Lighthouse on Eileen Musdile on the starboard side, and the green contours of Lismore, that fertile limestone island where my pony Ross was born in the year 2000. Now on the port side was the Isle of Mull where Shuna's pony, Chief, was born in 2010. The ferry trip was taking us past their birthplaces. It hadn't occurred to me until then that the ponies, now in an Ifor Williams horsebox on the vehicle deck below us, were both islanders.

I stood on the stern deck for a long time. The engine's vibrations travelled up through my feet to the tangle of nerves under

3

my ribcage. The air smelt of salt and diesel. As we came to the end of the Sound of Mull, Ardnamurchan Lighthouse snuck into sight on the point. To the west the isles of Rum, Eigg and Muck hunkered down on the horizon. Rum's hills lifted in easy blue across the miles of sea. Ross is a Rum Highland pony with rare ancient bloodlines. These ponies were bred to be versatile, one of their jobs being to take deer carcasses off the hill. They were described by Dr Samuel Johnson in his 1775 *Journey to the Western Islands* as 'very small but of a breed eminent for beauty'. They have unique colour combinations: fox dun and silver dun, liver and mouse and biscuit dun too. Some have zebra stripes up their pasterns and eel stripes along their spines. Ross's passport states his colour as 'dappled chocolate'; his mane has blonde highlights and in summer you can see the dark dapples across his body. It may be myth, but some say the unusual colours come from stallions that swam ashore from Spanish Armada shipwrecks and bred with native ponies. I love to think of the Spanish horses mixing with the Scottish horses on this Atlantic seaboard. I also love to think of some of those shipwrecked horses having survived, and Ross carrying their blood all these centuries later. Chief is a bright silvery grey. They are a striking pair, but most important of all they are great travel companions. Ross's experience makes up for Chief's inexperience, and Chief's bravery bolsters Ross in moments of doubt.

We'd left the Sound of Mull behind and were now out in the Sea of Hebrides. The last time I'd made this crossing was ten years previously, in July 2007, with Martin and the children on our way back from a holiday on Barra. It had been a hot windless day and the crossing was smooth. We'd leaned over the railings as we sailed through a broth of Basking Sharks. The sea was alive with them, their black fins visible a long way into the distance, cutting through the glittering sea. Today there was no sign of them, but every now and again a great spear-billed Gannet glided past, quickening my pulse every time.

I found Shuna standing in the observation lounge. It was exhilarating up there, all that height and light and the views through 180° of glass. My feet stepped across the carpeted floor. There was a quiet reverence in the air with people dotted about, binoculars on tables, maps out, knees crossed.

'It's fascinating,' Shuna whispered, turning to me. 'The couples, I think they must be the Jaguar Club, and they're all in matching pairs. Look, over there, those two, angular and skinny, and this couple, bespectacled and round-faced, and these two,' her voice dropped even lower as she nodded towards the nearest couple, sitting with their long legs stretched out, 'they've both got hair that sticks out at the back, and matching socks.' We were both smiling. A woman walking past swayed suddenly as she lost her balance. 'Better than Alton Towers, this is,' she laughed, her face wide with delight. I recognised her from the ferry queue. She was in a camper van which had stood out; the rest of the queue was mostly made up of classic Jaguars, crouching convertibles with their soft-tops down, their curved panels gleaming suede green and pearl.

Will the owner of the pickup and horsebox please go to the front desk. The voice on the tannoy sounded serious.

'Shit, hope they're okay,' I said loudly. Faces turned to look at us as we made our unsteady way back down the steep stairs.

'It's nothing to worry about,' the steward said, 'just thought you might like to check on the ponies, seeing as it's such a long trip. It's going to get a bit rougher for the next couple of hours.'

'They're so nice on this boat,' Shuna said as we made our way down another two steep flights of stairs to the vehicle deck.

'Look at that.' I reached out and touched her arm. From

5

where we stood we could see into the trailer. Chief had his head over in Ross's side of the box. They were both resting, cheek to cheek, ears touching.

I opened the side door and two sets of dark eyes looked down at us. It was warm in the box and the windows were steamed up, we breathed in the earth-sweet smell of horse and haylage. It struck us both then, that we were really doing this, we were on the boat out to Barra, the four of us. My eyes were swimming as I closed the drop-latches.

Back at our table in the dining area I scanned the sea. I'd never seen so many Dolphins, lines and lines of them coming towards us in leaps of slate-dark joy. 'A calf!' I looked to where Shuna was pointing, her face showing pure delight. The calf was in a line of about ten adults, bounding towards us broadside to the boat. She was her mother's half-size shadow, matching her fin for fin, eye for eye. Then they were almost beneath us and their underbellies glowed pale amber in the sunshine as they dived, backs shining in perfect arcing alignment.

My heart raced. There we were, high above the plimsoll line, Ross and Chief below us in their tilting trailer, and these Dolphins swimming through the sea beneath them. I thought about horses that had travelled on other boats in past centuries, and remembered why horses in the Americas were so extraordinary. Because only the fittest had survived the gruelling sea voyage from Spain, suspended in slings, living on rancid water and weevil-infested feed. The trust of horses constantly astonishes me. They would have followed their handlers along gangplanks, down into a swaying dark hold where they would have sickened and often died. The survivors would have stepped out onto new land, probably emaciated, but alive and prepared to face whatever their handlers asked of them.

Resting my chin on my hands, I remained without moving

for a long time as the boat started to roll more steeply. Shuna, wisely, had already lain down on the dining area floor. Now I didn't dare move. It was that critical stage where the slightest change can tip the balance of seasickness from uncomfortable to sick-bag stage. I'm a coward with nausea. My parents separated when I was two, and travel sickness was connected to high emotion from then onwards. I can still recall the nauseous feeling of being at the airport in Accra. I would have been three when Mum and my brothers and I left my father in Ghana where he worked at a veterinary aid project. Then there were long car trips with Dad when he was back on leave, and the sailing trips with him. I never did find my sea legs. When Dad came back from Africa for good there were car trips to the halfway meeting point between Argyll and Dumfries and Galloway, usually the car park outside the Little Chef at Dumbarton. I'd inherited travel sickness from Mum, who understood how being touched was the last thing you wanted when you were being sick. North of Dumbarton Dad would put his hand on my back when he stopped for me to be sick in this lay-by or that lay-by. I never asked him to take his hand away though.

I heard a commotion of seabirds and opened my eyes. The surface of the sea was pixelated with silver Sprats and above was a stramash of feeding seabirds. Dad would know what those birds were. If he was here, he'd be out on the deck, binoculars up, watching intently. How many years had it been since I stood on a CalMac deck, or sat on a wet bench in his Drascombe Lugger, listening to him naming birds: 'Kittiwake, fulmar, storm petrel.' Hearing how his voice would lighten, understanding that birds made him happy, and knowing how happy that made me. I promised myself to make more of an effort to see him when I got back from this trip. Looking down at the shadows of the lifeboats in the surf below, I closed my eyes and squeezed my hands together, as if closing them around

7

time itself, stopping the slippage. Surf bulged against the side of the ferry as nausea reeled through me.

Oban was five and a half hours and ninety odd miles behind us. Shuna and I were back out on deck with the islands of Muldonaich and Vatersay on the portside and Barra on the starboard. As the ferry turned smoothly into Castlebay, three Arctic Terns serrated the air with their cries as they swooped to the sea, trailing their forked tails behind them. These three 'sea swallows' had just made it back from their wintering grounds in the Antarctic, ten thousand miles, now *that* was a journey.

Kisimul Castle, on its rock in the bay, was lit up in sunshine. The hill behind it, Heaval, was black in cloud shadow. Not even the marble statue of the Madonna and child was visible today, but the Church of Our Lady of the Sea made up for it, resplendent in sunlight in the village below. I can't see Roman Catholic icons and churches without thinking of Mum. She had burst out of a convent when she was eighteen and made up for a crushing and abusive education every second of the rest of her life. I'd set out on this trip with a purse full of beads and a belief that what I needed to do was make my peace with her, but I would come to realise that I'd already done that when she was dying from the brain tumour that slowly took everything away from her. Only the quick-fire in her eyes stayed until the very end. She had died on a night with a full moon that shone hard and bright as platinum, which was somehow fitting for a woman who was full-hearted and flinty-sharp in equal measure. Yes, I had made my peace with her in those terrible winter-thin months. It was myself I needed to make peace with now. The regrets around our relationship were still grabbing at the back of my throat, still making it hard for me to breathe sometimes.

Scanning the darkened hillside for the white lady, I could hear Mum talking with passion about the Roman Catholic Church,

8

the cruelty of the nuns, the hypocrisy of the priests. What else would you expect from a religion that believes animals don't have souls, she'd say bitterly. I had taken this to heart and always felt uncomfortable around the rituals: the robes, mass, confession. I'd heard too many stories of what went on behind closed doors, the cruelty suffered by Mum in the convents she'd gone to, and by her two brothers in their boarding schools with the 'brothers'. Yet, at the very end, she'd chosen to have a rosary on her bedside table. My mother, so full of contradictions, always surprising. I hope it brought her comfort but, for me, I carry a prejudice. I shiver at religious iconography. My chest tightens when I see a nun's habit, a priest's collar. I am an animist through and through. That is where I find my God, in the natural world. In the birds and animals and frosts and mosses, and in the humanity of our own animal being.

*Would owners of all vehicles please make their way
to the vehicle deck.*

On the way down we stopped to take a photograph of a pinned notice: *THE PEOPLE OF BARRA WELCOME ALL VISTORS. HOWEVER, THE FOLLOWING RULES WILL APPLY:* Rule number four read: THE SPEED LIMIT IS 60mph NOT 30mph. Beneath our shared amusement we were both anxious, and worried about traffic. Chief was very inexperienced and, although Ross was fairly confident, I had my own issues around traffic. To be honest, I found riding on the roads terrifying. People had been warning us that this year the island roads were busier than ever, even this early in the season.

As we drove up the hill I looked in the side mirror. The last vehicle to disembark was a red quad bike, the same colour as the funnels on the ferry towering above it, a raw brave red. In front of it was one of the classic Jaguars, azure and flawless as the sky overhead. That picture. Right there. Utter perfection. I turned to face forwards again and let out a 'whoop' as we drove past the sign *Failte. Live it. Visit Hebrides.*

'You must be Shuna,' said the woman standing at the driver's window. 'How was the crossing? How are the ponies?' She rattled off questions. Naomi had pulled over in front of us when we'd stopped to get our bearings. 'I've been keeping an eye out for you. Not too many horseboxes come off this ferry.' She was laughing and her ponytail whipped round in the wind. Naomi, a friend of a friend of a friend, had pre-arranged for us to camp on the common grazing at Tangasdale Machair in the south-west corner of the island.

'Follow me, I'll show you where to go.'

When we took their halters off, both ponies lifted their heads and sniffed the air. Ross led Chief off to explore, swinging his head from side to side, the great pony explorer. In the evening light we agreed they looked magnificent, lit up from inside and out. We loved seeing them like this. Loose-limbed they set off, adventure and newness defined their muscles, altered the lift of their necks. We found a sheltered spot out of the wind and, after arranging to meet Naomi later, set up camp. Every now and again the ponies would come back to our camping spot, a hollow where the machair sward merged into marram grass, and grazed distractedly on the new grass that was just starting to show. Then they would canter off once more in wild mustang mode.

Once the tent was up, sleeping mats and bags in, we decided to have a look at the beach and walked with the ponies along sandy paths strewn with empty, sun-bleached snail shells. The air was a-spin with the chatter of Starlings. Ross's mane and the marram were the same sun-on-straw colour, both being flicked seaward by the wind. On the beach the ponies' soft footfall joined the soundscape of the Oystercatchers' and Common Gulls' commotion-at-dusk and, higher up, like a stitch being pulled in the evening sky, the call of Geese.

A woman and a dog approached us from the north end of the bay. 'Hello, do you mind if he meets the ponies? He's just a pup, he's interested…' She told us he was a red and white setter. Not a breed either of us knew, he was stringy and windblown and all ears and tongue-lolling delight.

'I've been here nearly a week,' said the hatted and scarfed woman, her shoulders pulled up towards her ears, 'and I'm shattered by the wind.' I felt the sincerity of her words. Chief, like the clouds, was limned by the dropping sun. Silver strokes flashed along his top-line, the curve of his ear, tangled in his whiskers and tail. The rest of his body was in near-darkness, his sand-shadow stretched away from the sea back towards the dunes, the machair and the hill where a single salmon-pink roof stood out against the pearly rock.

Later, in the warmth of Naomi's house overlooking Castlebay, with mugs of strong tea in our hands, we heard a little of the life she shared with her son and husband, their multiple jobs including veterinary supplies dispenser and firefighter at the airport, and their many animals. Those animals were at the centre of their world. A Norwegian Forest Cat and Tibetan Mastiff puppy absorbed the living room in precious long-haired splendour, and over the fireplace was a picture of Naomi's three horses, looking down at us from a rock on the hill, rulers of their world.

That night we lay listening to Oystercatchers piping outside and the wind tugging at the tent as we passed the hip flask back and forth. We had a lot to celebrate. By dawn we'd put on every item of clothing we had with us, including coats, hats and buffs.

It was Baltic, the tent and sleeping bags had come short of the mark. We'd bought the spring/summer range; autumn/winter would have been more suitable. It was the first of many uncomfortable nights, yet the magic of being there together was inextinguishable. In the night the ponies galloped by the tent and I wondered if I was dreaming, but the *boran*-beat of their hooves on the machair and the racket of disturbed Oystercatchers were more real than even my wildest, most vivid dreams.

DAY TWO

Tangasdale Machair to Eoligarry

Packing away the tent was like trying to put a feral cat into a bag. The wind was sending the light fabric into a frenzy when I was ragged with lack of sleep. We worked quietly and quickly, spots of rain pinging our skin, that weighty grey sky was about to let rip.

'Good job we've got the horsebox this morning,' Shuna said with feeling. The rain pummelling on the metal roof syncopated with the soft hiss of the gas stove. Steam bloomed on the inside of the window while on the outside fat raindrops smeared the Marram Grass into a leaden sky. There was no sign of the ponies so we guessed they'd found a sandy hollow to shelter in and were standing side by side, heads down, bums to the rain and wind.

Shuna carefully sliced a banana into our porridge. 'Honey?' she asked. I nodded and sat on a plastic-wrapped haylage bale. Luxury. Most nights, camping would be without the trailer. The rough plan as we rode up the islands was to drive the pickup and trailer to the next ferry crossing, leave it there and hitch a lift back to the ponies. Or ride first, and hitch back to collect the vehicle. Either way would require some leapfrogging and a willingness to go with the flow. On other trips we'd had everything organised in advance: daily itineraries; each night's accommodation sorted; drop offs planned; and food parcels sent ahead. This time, since we needed the trailer to get the ponies onto each ferry, we'd decided to make the most of that extra space. We had a chest full of food: tins of sardines, smoked oysters and mussels, a few camping-ready meals, bags of couscous and pasta, dark chocolate, whisky, coffee, Earl Grey teabags, Nairn's oatcakes, hunks of cheese, packets of Naked bars, porridge oats, honey and raisins, salted peanuts and cashews. We definitely wouldn't starve. We also had a case of Prosecco and six half-bottles of Oban whisky to give as gifts.

When Shuna handed me a cup of porridge, I noticed my resistance but was determined to be a porridge eater on this trip. Mum had loved her porridge, but she'd made hers with full-fat milk and lavished it with double cream and brown sugar. No salt and water for her. In the horsebox that morning I managed to eat almost all of my porridge before any thoughts of gagging snuck in. Perhaps the success was down to my spork. Having shopped, planned, prepared for this trip for a long time, we had all the camping gear. The tiny foldable gas stove was Shuna's pride and joy, crouching steady on its stainless steel lobster legs on the sawdust-strewn floor. As well as being a professional horse trainer Shuna also works as a cook. Her organisation around food is fabulous. This is great for me, and for my food anxiety. The thought of running out has always sent me into a panic. I have no reason for this, I've never been food deprived. We may not have had treats when I was growing up, there was never any spare money, but there was always food. Mum did funny things around food though. She'd have butter that was *only for her*, the rest of us had margarine, and chocolate that was *only for her*. She had a good excuse, having been perpetually hungry in boarding school, in the convents in Wales, England and

Belgium. Other children's parents would send goody parcels. Hers hadn't, I never asked why, but the result was that food, especially her own 'special treats', had been very important to her. Perhaps some of her anxiety had rubbed off on me.

The strong aroma of coffee mingled with the fresh wood shavings and yesterday's horse dung, three smells that filled me with a deep sense of well-being. The tiny new Bialetti was perfect for slipping into a saddlebag. Lifting its lid I saw the last of the coffee bubble up. Our hearts got lively with caffeine and the rain battered on. We weren't in any hurry, having only seven miles to ride that day and were happy to wait and see if the rain would pass. We brought our gear in from the pickup, packed our saddlebags, looked at the map and folded it into the waterproof case, had another coffee. Then the sun pressed a golden light through the clouds which, from one moment to the next, transformed the morning.

At the burn to wash the pots, I found each wet stem of marram grass was balancing light like a sword edge. A drake Mallard flew over, his head a startle of tourmaline. I cleaned the pots with strands of sheep's wool that I found caught on the fence. Judging by the lines of dark Bladderwrack tangled along its base it got regular batterings by the sea. The fence was a work of art, patched with zigzags of baler twine holding the upper strand of barbed wire to the Rylock below. Some of the twine was orange, some was yellow, and the crisscrossing seemed perfectly symmetrical between the fence posts that leant in all angles from their volatile sandy base. I have always had a thing about gate and fence repairs and my eye picks them out everywhere I go. I like to imagine the minds behind the hands that mended. I like to see the layers of time and weathering made visible by each twist of wire, knot of string, breadth of rope. The ingenuity and creativity always delights me, but I'd never seen such decisive zigzagging as this before. The colours

17

were synthetic and strident, but even they weren't resistant to the weathering. Fibres that had twisted awry of the main body of twine had faded to translucence. Mum would have appreciated this fence: its withstanding, its refusal to be beaten.

I took the bead purse out of my pocket. It was wet. My Ebay-bought Gortex jacket hadn't stood up to the drive of the rain earlier. I unzipped the purse and looked inside and the moment suddenly sat heavily on me. A memory of a morning in Oban and Islands District Hospital, turning to wave goodbye to Mum from the ward door, seeing her face brightening.

'You said the words,' she'd said, in a smalling voice from the bed.

'What?' I'd answered.

'You said *I love you.*'

I ran a hand through the water that flowed topaz-coloured down from Loch Tangasdale, and settled for two beads: a smooth oval wooden one and a second ceramic one that was irregularly shaped and glazed in a bold metallic bronze. Carefully threading them onto a length of the silk string, I twisted it onto the upper strand of wire, making sure a barb kept the two beads separate. The bronze bead rested beneath the wire next to a triangulated summit of orange baler twine. The wooden bead rested on top of the wire. I was satisfied, and wondered if the crofter would find them as he or she made their next round of repairs, or if they'd make it to the sea, or fall to the sand, before being seen by a human again.

We were looking for Chief. We'd found Ross alone by the roadside fence being petted by walkers, he was walking beside me now through the dunes. Every now and again he'd stop and lift his head and call out a high-pitched neigh, his whole body vibrating with tremors that carried along the rope to my hand, up my arm, into my body. The three of us listened for a reply but couldn't hear anything above the wind. Shuna was quiet. It doesn't take long for the imagination to go into overdrive: Chief's legs caught in wire, Chief escaped and gone for miles, Chief swimming out to sea, Chief stolen. We followed sets of hoof tracks through the dunes where they'd been galloping in the night. Down on the beach the tracks thinned to just one set of hoof prints which led to the far end of the bay. There the fence line ended a little short of the sea, and if he really wanted to, a pony could cross the rocks and head up onto the hill. Shuna set off at a run. Ten minutes later we met her and Chief coming back round the shoreline.

'He was so pleased to see me! Don't know what he was doing round there, but he's fine. He's totally fine.' Relief lightened her face.

We'd left the road and were riding down a grassy track to the burial ground on the point at Borve Point. The ponies were striding out, looking all around them, their hooves making soft thuds on the sandy soil. We passed a sheep track that trickled through the machair to a single standing stone, clearly a favoured rubbing post. There was a long fenced off potato strip, the sandy soil piled up in neat ridges, tattie shaws just starting to show. Then, between Ross's ears, a huddle of crosses showed up on the skyline against a pewter sea. They were all facing eastwards, to us and to the rising sun. The graveyard was enclosed by a tall dry-stone dyke. It had fallen down in places and the ubiquitous strands of barbed wire were strung across the gaps, ribbons of last year's silage bale wrap fluttered in the wind like Tibetan prayer flags. A plaited fisherman's rope lay in recumbent coils between the dyke and the shore. It was melded into the shoreline, its hemp spirals sewn through with Moss and Silverweed. Alongside it, boulders that had rolled from the wall were embossed in yolk-yellow Lichen, cat's-tongue rough to the touch.

We got off and led the ponies to a gate on the far side of the burial ground. A sign told us it was a Commonwealth graveyard, that casualties from both the First and Second World Wars were buried here. We took it in turns to hold the ponies while the other wandered amongst the stones, listening, touching, reading. The lettered, dated summations of lives, short-lived and long-lived, were being taken over by Lichens, some like smooth spillages of cream, others sage-green and wiry. The air was strung with the oscillating calls of Curlews, and Lapwings flung themselves in somersaults against the wind. This place of remembrance was a sanctuary for birds. I felt a sense of privilege to be there that was almost too much to bear. We walked in silence towards the tip of the point, the carved gravestones replaced by body-sized rocks left by the sea, or glaciers, or maybe both. A Curlew whistled in alarm and we stopped. The sky was full of birds watching over their nests, we had a sense of trespassing on hallowed ground. The bird calls escalated, echoing our own sense of wonder. As we retreated a slender head and neck peered at us from above a rock, there was something strangely adolescent about this bird as it wheeled up, all awkward elegance before the sky stole it. Later, the bird book told us it was a Godwit.

We walked back in the lee of the wall. Underfoot was a mixture of dried cow dung and sand, a refuge for cattle in the winter months. As we left quietly through the gate, its metal rungs holey with rust, an Arctic Tern trailed its long tail with impossible grace in the air above us. *Shapeshifter,* I thought, as a fine rain blew across our faces.

The Curlews' spiralling calls had tuned me in to a world tilting ever-so-slightly differently on its axis, a world I wanted to know more deeply, and one I'd need to learn a new language to explore. Shuna had told me, down at the graveyard, that Karen Matheson, her sister-in-law, had family buried there. Karen's mother had left Barra when she was sixteen to go and work in the hotels in Oban. She had been ashamed of her Gaelic, as many were at that time, and hadn't spoken it in the home. In spite of this, or perhaps because of it, Karen had gone on to become a world-renowned Gaelic singer, forming the band Capercaillie with Shuna's brother Donald Shaw, and becoming an impassioned ambassador for the language. Her last album was a return to her Hebridean roots, recording traditional songs and poems. 'Urram', the Gaelic for 'respect' and 'honour'. Urram, what a beautiful word.

'Look, I can post my cards.' We were back on the tarmac road and Shuna was pointing to the postbox on the verge ahead. As she leant over and posted from the saddle, delight spreading across her face, I laughed at the improbability of it all. At us Michelin women padded out in full waterproofs, our faces red-ruddy from the wind. At the two glossy postcards sent on their way at the end of a quiet township road on Barra.

As the road cut inland the surge of beryl sea on our left was replaced by fields and stock fences. In places each barb on the wire was coated in sorrel cattle hair, like felted pearls. 'Allasdale,' said Shuna, looking at a road sign ahead. 'I read what that means: *elves' milking place*, from the Norse'. I imagined them nipping in and milking the cattle, their fair dues. For what, I wondered.

We settled into a rhythm of looking behind and in front for traffic, measuring the distances to the next passing places or stepping off the road when there was room to let a car pass. The drivers slowed down, and smiling, interested faces looked out from passing pickups, cars, the post-van. There was also a steady flow of camper vans, but we got the feeling they were trying to make amends for their size and boxy ugliness with extra sensitive driving. Just as we were beginning to feel more confident about the traffic our complacency was shattered.

Riding up a steep incline, where the road crosses over from the west side of the island to the east, between two hills, a bin lorry came over the skyline. It slowed down, but as it passed its hydraulic brakes hissed. Chief panicked, tried to turn and run back towards Ross and me but there was no room, so he leapt over the ditch on the left. Shuna had jumped off but had fallen in the ditch. In a nightmarishly slow-motion sequence, we were both aware of the tangled mess of old fence wire on the other side of the ditch, of the panicking pony, of the dark underbelly of the lorry, of all the things that could go wrong. By this time the shocked-looking driver had stopped. It wasn't his fault. We shouldn't have been so blasé. Chief is a young horse and we had expected too much of him. We should have asked the lorry to stop while we trotted back to a passing place where there was room to get well out of the way.

The lorry left, rattling into the distance. Shuna was picking bits of bramble off herself. She and Chief were shaken, but unhurt. Meanwhile, I was in helpless fits of giggles. Not because I thought it was funny, as it clearly wasn't, but because I have an unfortunate response to shock sometimes. I've been known to burst into giggles at the news that someone has just died. I remember Mum doing something similar at my stepfather's funeral, twenty years ago in the Crematorium in Ayr. We were all waiting to go in for the service, and there was Mum, joking with her best friend, stifling laughter. My brothers and I were mortified, his three grown children sitting silently opposite. Paul, their father, and our stepfather for the last sixteen years, had hanged himself ten days previously.

'I'm sorry, Shuna, I'm sorry...are you okay?' My voice cracked on another wave of giggles. I knew she would understand they were coming from a place of distress. It wasn't the first time she'd seen me do this.

'Let's keep walking,' she said, knowing the best way for horses to get past trauma is movement. As we walked my giggles ebbed away. Thank God Chief and Shuna were okay. What could have happened back there didn't bear thinking about. I found myself remembering Mum's own funeral in Clydebank Crematorium. I hadn't giggled then. Not once. Not even a belly-tickle hint of it. None of us had giggled on the trip down from Oban in Will's Ford Transit minibus. Nine of us: Martin and I, our daughter Brèagha, my brothers Will and Tom and their partners, and Dad. I will be eternally grateful for his presence that day. Christine was also there, a spiritual healer who Mum had been seeing in the five years she'd been living in Argyll. Once, when she was in the care home and still able to talk, I had walked in on a session. Christine gestured for me to sit down, and I listened as she guided Mum through a visualisation of a 'safe place' that she had obviously visited before. Mum described the 'friend' who waited for her there, a grey mare. Tears rolled down my face, suddenly seeing how little of her I'd known.

On the day of her funeral we met Mum's friend Moira, and her partner, Pete, at the crematorium. They had driven up from Yorkshire in a convertible with broken windscreen wipers through sleet and rain. There were eleven of us in all, so few people at the end of such a full life, and all looked shattered. It was the 24th of December 2010. There was an icy fog in Dumbarton and I remember how when we came out of the crematorium the sun broke through and a single Robin started singing, splitting the cold December air into galaxies of notes.

Up ahead, a track went off to the right, through a gate, and alongside Loch an Dùirn. It looked like a good place to stop and we needed to get away from the traffic. We got the stove out and had tea, oatcakes and sardines. It was Barra's rush hour. The camper vans thinned out and cement lorries, pickups and nippy cars drove past in a sudden and steady stream. A car pulled into the gateway, and a woman with a young boy got out and walked towards us.

'Is it okay if we pet the ponies?' She and her son lived in the 'Millennium Houses down the hill'. Apparently, Prince Charles had designed them. We'd noticed them earlier, anachronistic in a cul-de-sac curve, a raised eyebrow on the hillside. The woman was interested in where we'd come from and where we were going. While we chatted, her son held gentle hands to the ponies' muzzles. He didn't say a word.

'Ah, Tangasdale, that's *my* common. The wee house up the hill, did you see it? My grandfather built it. He had the Horses too, and my dad. They worked with them. They both had a way with them.' The woman pointed to the track where it disappeared into the hills. 'That's where they'd bring the peats down from.' She was silent as we looked up at the dark ground. 'My dad used to say that up there,' she was pointing into the hill-buckled heart of the island, 'that's where it all goes on, the standing stones, the ghosts.'

We watched the little car drive away, and were left wondering, what *it all* was.

It was late in the day when we arrived at the Airport beach, Tràigh Mhòr, on the north east of the island. The tide was out and the windsocks were down; no more aeroplane landings on the beach today. The shaley sand stretched out for miles.

We took the hoof boots off the ponies as they wouldn't be needing them any more today, and stepped over the bright shell sand to the ripple marks that overlapped like fish scales through a thin film of water. Vehicle tracks shone in straight lines across the tidal flats and, in the distance, we saw cars and tiny figures, cockle pickers. I remembered being here with Martin and the children eight years previously. They'd been ten, eight and six. It was a cloudless day and the children, all bright blonde back then, had guddled in the sand in bare feet and bare legs. The three of them spread out, coming back with clutches of Cockles, some as big as their palms, grooved and heart-shaped. We ate a lot of Cockles on that holiday. Razor Clams too that we'd caught at low tide on the east beach on Vatersay.

Today the sky was low and grey, but to the north, where we were headed, it was marbled with blue. The ponies' manes lifted in the wind as they stepped lightly and loosely over the reflected sky, and the insides of my cheeks tightened with enjoyment at the sound of swashing hooves and the dense smell of the salty strand.

'Let's come and gallop on the beach tomorrow, when we don't have any saddlebags,' said Shuna. My heart raced in response.

The man in a hi-vis jacket dropped Cockles into his bucket. It was the same duck-beak yellow as his wellies. I recognised the bucket. We have them at home, the sheep's mineral licks come in them. Yellow is an easy colour to spot on the hill, easy to spot on the beach too. He leant on his rake as we approached.

'I do it for the exercise,' he explained, 'just fill one bucket when I'm not working.' He worked on the Eriskay ferry. 'One week on, one week off.'

I waved my hands towards the other cockle pickers. 'Are the Cockles decreasing?' I asked.

'Well, they used to dredge it with tractors, but they're barred now. All done by hand. No, they'll never run out, the beach is too big.' I savoured his sense of scale, his optimism, as my eyes picked out the little islands of raised sand where he'd been with his rake. We said goodbye and rode on.

We headed towards the bar of sandy horizon between the township of Eoligarry where we were staying that night, and the uninhabited tidal island of Orosay. We could see the hills of Fuday, Eriskay and South Uist under the faraway drifts of blue sky, and passed a man and a woman with a wheelbarrow, hard at the cockling, nodding their heads at us without pausing in their work. Nearby was a pile of four nylon-net sacks, leaning in towards each other, each one packed to the gunnels with rose-ochre Cockles. We rode through a tractor graveyard, a concoction of corrosion, rufous-red angles and curves, rusting iron layered like filo pastry. I felt a pang for all that past horse-power sinking slowly into the sand. The beach at Orosay was made of whole shells, Cockles and Razor Clams that snapped underfoot. Gulls noisily relayed our arrival and wheeled over the grassy island. We stopped there for a few awe-stretched minutes before wading belly-deep through a tidal channel and heading west towards Eoligarry.

'I'm not sure where Richard's house is, but we can ask,' said Shuna, passing me the hip flask. We hadn't met Richard, but through Shuna's sister-in-law, Karen, he had kindly offered us his house for a couple of nights. As we left the beach via a green-flanked sandy track, a man waved and shouted hello from the road.

'I'm Rob,' he said. 'I've been looking out for you.' A friend of Richard's, he had sandy hair and a radiant smile and had a croft where we could put the ponies. Shuna had arranged all this in advance and, once again, I felt a surge of appreciation for all the planning she'd done. We followed Rob's instructions along a single-track road, through crofts vibrating with the courting call of male Corncrakes, past gates and fences sculpted out of bed-ends and fish crates and ropes of all colours, and of course baler twine, lots and lots of baler twine. From the glances we exchanged I could tell we both already loved this place.

'Rob's croft must be over there.' Shuna pointed at some trees on the skyline. He'd told us to look out for the trees they'd planted. 'Olearia, from New Zealand, they can withstand the salt.'

The field hadn't been grazed for a while and there was a good bite of grass. We walked down over a bank smudged in pale yellow Primroses. I had never seen so many in one place before. Beyond the fence the marram-bank dropped steeply into a biscuity band of sand. Beyond that a strip of turquoise sea losing itself eventually to the aubergine hue of the South Uist hills. I bent down and picked a single petal from a Primrose and put it in my mouth, the gentle flavour summed up the subtle-sweet essence of this place. Next to the field, and nestled in amongst the trees, was a wooden hut – with its silvering larch cladding and dove-grey tin roof it was a natural extension of all that sky and sea and sand. We found a hose and filled a wheelbarrow for the ponies. They drank deeply.

Rob picked us up in his white Land Rover. 'The same one we had when we lived in Africa,' he told us warmly. '1993, 300 TDI, assembled in Zimbabwe.' It had green canvas safari seats and you could almost smell the dust and dreams and adventure in their seams.

'There's Angus John wanting a word,' he said as he pulled alongside a large man in overalls filling water troughs and surrounded by perky-faced black Cattle.

'Now then, what about these ponies, they won't be escaping, will they?' Angus John said, coming to the fence and getting straight to the point.

'No, I think they'll be fine,' Shuna said. 'They look very happy where they are.' There was a pause.

'And what would you do if they did?' he added, clearly not too impressed with our reassurances. 'I've just planted my potatoes.'

'They don't call him "the bear" for nothing,' Rob said, smiling, as we drove away.

The whole of the east side of the house was glass. Shuna and I looked out across the bay towards Orosay and the islands of

Hellisay and Gighay with Eriskay beyond. Something tiny was meandering across the bay towards us.

'It's someone on a bike,' I said incredulously as it got closer. We sat watching the bike weave drunkenly over the sand. As it came closer, we saw it was a man riding one-handed. With the other he was holding a full sack of Cockles, an almost impossible feat of balance we imagined.

'If I lived in this house I'd spend my life right here, just sitting, looking out of this window,' Shuna said. The view would never be the same twice. It would be ever-changing with the tides and weather and light. 'But we'd better get going,' she continued, standing beside a telescope as tall as she was. Rob and Kate had invited us over for supper. It wouldn't be a hardship to leave our couscous in the saddlebag tonight. Nothing was a hardship. We had landed in the lap of luxury.

Over dinner Rob talked both of his lifelong Rhinoceros conservation work in Africa, and his more recent work with re-wilding in Scotland. It turned out that his mother owned *Taigh Cialla*, a house on the point opposite Orosay, and he had spent his childhood holidays there. Rob and Kate and their own children still stayed there each year. With no electricity it was a time to 'just be' in this wonderful place, a time to connect with their now-adult children and others in the family. But this was a working trip and they needed the internet so were renting this cottage nearby. They came up to Barra from Cambridge as often as they could and would be here until the end of June.

'My mother was widowed in the war,' Rob told us. 'She came back in a convoy from India with her baby, and landed in Glasgow Docks. *Taigh Cialla* belonged to her husband's family. She started writing this diary in 1945,' he said, getting up and going over to a bookshelf. He placed the book carefully on the table. Written by hand above a grainy photograph of the house was *Taigh Rudha Chialla*. Below, in small typeface, *by Joan Diana Brett*. On the first page, beneath a faded watercolour seascape, lines of careful handwriting rippled across the page.

'THE HOUSE stands on a low grassy promontory bordered by rocks. Rhudha Chialla, which reaches out to the tidal island of Orosay. On either side are great white cockle strands, Traigh Mhor to the south, Traigh Cille Barra to the east, covered at high tide for nearly a mile...'

We turned the pages with wine-edged delight.

'There are forty crofts in Eoligarry, and the crofters' cattle graze the hills and the machair, a fine lime-rich sward covered with primroses and other wild flowers in spring and summer. But this pasture is much depleted by rabbits, who thrive in their thousands and undermine the sandy soil. The forty crofting families of Eoligarry mostly do little crofting now, apart from cattle rearing, potato growing, but cockle gathering is now profitable again, and people are out on the strand every low tide, raking them up – some of them have fishing boats, fast and Diesel-powered, which go round the north point of Scurrival most days to work lobster creels out on the west side...'

Shuna pointed to a photo titled Barra ponies. There must have been two dozen, including foals, walking across the sands, their reflections intact in the still pools of water left by the tide.

'Rob and I met on that beach when we were eighteen,' Kate said. Her wide smile showed that theirs was a marriage still gathering momentum after all these decades. As he'd been doing all evening, off and on, Rob was back at the window with his binoculars. He didn't say what he was looking for, but his watchful stance was imbued with fascination and love for this place.

After dinner, Kate took us up into the loft to see the workshop where she made a specialist marbling paper used in bookbinding and lampshade making. We ducked our head under sheets of paper pegged in lines beneath the low coombed ceiling. The process involves carrageen seaweed, which was used to make the jelly the paint floated on.

She poured this Carrageen into a shallow tray and with her small neat hands used a brush to drop in paint, naming the colours like an incantation as she went. Using a knitting needle and combs she created patterns on the surface before gently laying down and lifting a sheet of paper: lichen spatters on rock, curves of white and sorrel shell, sand ripples under thin sea, frayed edges of the whelming tide. It was all there on the wet paper, and on the others hanging pegged and crispy-edged: papery worlds rendered in indigo, cadmium red, yellow ochre, burnt sienna. Shuna and I looked at each other in astonishment.

We left holding precious samples of *French Shell* and *Antique Spot* lightly between our fingers, climbed the stile to Richard's house and listened to the Corncrakes rasping into the opening night. A single sun-splash of gold held fast to the sky.

DAY THREE
Exploring Eoligarry

'Beady, come on,' Shuna shouted up the stairs, 'they'll be here in ten minutes, time for a cup of tea if you're quick.'

Rob and Kate had offered us a lift back to Tangasdale to collect the pickup and trailer. Kate sat in the front of the Land Rover with one arm around several long brown tubes resting on her lap. Each had a handwritten address label, each contained marbled paper on its way to specialist bookbinders. We followed the road past the airport. The tide was out again, and I felt suddenly wide awake seeing that expanse of sand we'd ridden across yesterday. We drove past the tiny shell-lucent bay, where we'd taken the ponies' boots off, and slowed before overtaking a bicycle laden with sacks of cockles. A broad-shouldered man was pushing it, and a woman walked on the other side, one hand steadying the bike.

'That's the Romanian family,' said Kate, 'on their way with today's cockles.' At Northbay she pointed out a small wooded gully beyond a kissing gate, saying there were some lovely oak trees in there.

'And that's John Pendry's croft,' Rob said, nodding to a thickly wooded area on the other side of the road. 'He planted every single one of those trees. His house is completely hidden in there now.' I loved Kate and Rob's shared delight in the island's scarce and precious woodland.

We turned right at the scramble of signs I'd marvelled at the day before: 'Castlebay via east', 'Castlebay via west', 'Barra Airport', 'Eoligarry', 'Sound of Barra Ferry', all with their Gaelic counterparts. Others were only in English: 'Hebridean Way', 'Croft Number 2 Campsite', 'Mingulay Boat Trips', 'Barra Bike Hire'. We drove up the hill alongside Northbay Community Woodland – when we'd ridden here yesterday the scent of Bluebells had engulfed us – on past the old water mill, and Loch an Dùin where we'd had our post-traffic-panic picnic. Waving his hand towards a small stone bridge Rob told us that if we followed the river we'd get to Loch an Eich Uisge, the loch of the water horse. Local lore tells how the water horse would appear in the shape of a handsome man to entrap his female victims and lure them to a watery death. Then we were travelling down the steep hill past a boat high and dry in a cradle, past an old house crumbling delicately, its slates slipping onto the hillside.

We were nearly back at Tangasdale, where the banks of a burn had been built entirely of Scallop shells. I'd never seen so many in one place. I'd taken photos the day before of the gabians holding hundreds in place, their fluted edges sanded smooth by the weather. Shells like these still held the thrill of childhood for me, the draw of their size, tones of pink, the creamy white grooves inside. I remembered collecting them when I was small. When we came back from Africa Mum worked for a seafood export company on Anglesey. We'd sit for hours and hours in the car. 'Wait there, children, I won't be long,' she'd say. Invariably she was. We'd get out and explore, collect scallop shells, treasure, some weathered and clean, some with little buttons of flesh still at the hinge. The whole place had stunk sweetly of a smell that still takes me back to a time when I doted on my mother.

I can almost touch the sense of her I had in my chest, then, when I was little and the biggest, most important, thing I knew was that love for my beautiful singing mother with her long red hair. I was always trying to catch her, and she was always slipping away. In the liminal time before a date, when she would be cheerful, listening to music, putting on her make-up, hurriedly putting us to bed, telling us to stay upstairs, she would tell us to 'behave for the Mondays', our babysitters. One of the teenage brothers would come over but, when they were there, I'd feel unsafe. Lying in my bed looking at the dark branches outside my bedroom window, the picture of a tiny red-hooded girl on my wall, I would ache for Mum to come home. The Mondays were scary, and to me most of Mum's boyfriends were scary. I'd get stomach cramps when left on my own with them, always.

Those were the years between Mum leaving Dad in 1975 and marrying Paul in 1981. Decades later I read these lines of Sylvia Plath's: 'Out of the ash I rise/With my red hair/And I eat men like air' and I thought 'that's Mum'. I'd loved and loved and loved her, in a bigger-than-me way, right up until I was in my teens. She was my role model and my idol and I hung on her words. I wrote gushing essays about her for English, but then she got sick.

It may be that around that time I would have gone through a natural disenchantment anyway, part of the 'individuating from the mother' that psychology books talk about. I wish it had just been that. A phase. Time to individuate. And then I could have found her again. But we never did really find one another again, not in a truly loving and accepting way. She had always made it clear she wanted us to leave home as soon as possible. I left at sixteen. I had been young for my year and had enough Highers for university. Perhaps she thought she was doing us a favour, and maybe she was, but it compounded my feelings of being unwanted and rootless. I'd been happy enough to leave though. Mum was very ill with a brain tumour, which my stepfather Paul blamed me for. 'This is all your fucking fault.' I think at some level I believed him. It was definitely easier to go than to stay.

Willie Mackay the farrier talked to me in the barn before I left home. He put a hind hoof down and looked over my shoulder towards the house, his face red with exertion, and said, 'She's the only mother you'll ever have.' I think he was advising me against my plan to go to Australia to be a cowgirl. I was going though, encouraged by Mum. Once I left, I never felt close and safe with her again. Not really. I tried. She tried. We both bloody tried, but it wasn't until she was dying, twenty-two years later, that I felt the unconditional love I'd had for her when I was little come back. It was agony and it was bliss, like blood coming back into frozen fingers. Feeling defensive and judged during all those years had been exhausting. Having hung on, white-knuckled, to stories that had served my insecurities, suddenly we were connecting again. I could let go, but I don't think the feeling of being judged ever left completely. Even at the end when she couldn't speak I would imagine the tracks of her scalpel-sharp thoughts, but I also saw that I might have been wrong. That maybe she was in a soft place. That finally, as she was dying, she could let her guard down. That it was safe for both of us to let our guards down.

As Rob and Kate's Land Rover rattled its way round the Barra bends I closed my eyes around that image of all those stacked scallop shells. The scallop shell, as Alastair McIntosh writes in his book *Poacher's Pilgrimage*, the story of his walk through Harris and Lewis, 'is the symbol of pilgrimage. Its radial ribs converge towards the hinge, like pilgrim paths all leading to the sacred place.' I was happy that our route through the Hebrides with the ponies wasn't fixed, and I hoped that every rib of the journey would in some way or another bend towards love. I still had so many regrets. I mourned that my brothers and I hadn't talked to Mum about her death while she could still speak. But we'd followed her lead. This woman who would speak about anything, anywhere, often toe-curlingly inappropriately, suddenly had an elephant in the room. Maybe she thought she was saving us from pain by not talking about it, as we thought we were saving her. Whatever way round, now it was hard to live with. I wish I could have heard her fears, her sadnesses, her joys. Instead, we talked small nonsenses, and then, one day, she couldn't speak any longer and, after that, she lay for months with eyes brimful of all the slippery unspoken words. I did tell her I loved her, over and over again, but nothing could make up for the lost years. 'Don't feel bad,' her friend Moira had said to me at her funeral, 'your mum was impossible,' but I did feel bad. I still felt bad. The farrier had been right. She was the only mother I'd ever have. She was there now though, enmeshed in who I was and who I had become, and I knew she was moving through me on this journey. I didn't know where it would take us, but it felt good to have started laying down a necklace for her through these shell-freckled islands.

We reconnected with the pickup and trailer and drove back along the east road, collecting some supplies in Castlebay on the way. Shuna had been anxious that we'd be short of fresh salad on our trip, but we needn't have worried. The Hebrides, it turned out, was the last glorious stronghold of the Co-operative. Outside the Co-op store were chunky recycling containers, the original forget-me-not blue paintwork hinting between welts of rust. I was taken by the writing on the side: *Comhairle nan Eilean Siar/ Working Together for the Western Isles/ Market Stance Waste Transfer Station/ Isle of Benbecula*. It wasn't until months later, when I read Terry J. Williams' book *Walking with Cattle: In Search of the Last Drovers of Uist*, that I learned that the Outer Hebrides had also been the last stronghold of cattle droving, and that they were still being walked to the ferries in the mid-sixties. There had been a string of sale stances through the Uists, and the Market Stance on Benbecula had been one of eight. Now they are mostly forgotten, or like this one, had undergone a change of use. I looked through the holes in the side of the nearest recycling container, all the way through to grey sky on the other side. *Glainne, Glass Only*. It would have to be a glass bead for Mum today.

In the community shop the smiling long-skirted woman told us that there was 'a ceilidh on in Northbay tonight, pot luck dinner, from 7pm, if you fancy it'. We did fancy it, but didn't want to make definite plans. In the fridge was some Barratlantic smoked salmon, produced by a shellfish seafood exporter based here on Barra. Possibly it was the same company Mum had dealings with. Several years and house-moves after working on Anglesey I remember her going off to Barra from where we lived in Dumfries and Galloway. She would be 'dressed to the nines' in tall leather boots and a suit, looking glorious.

We'd passed the sign to Barratlantic on the ponies the day before and I'd wondered if this was where she had come on those business trips. I'm sure there were ways I could have found out, but I enjoyed the fluidity of not-exactly-knowing. Over the next three weeks I would often find myself asking questions: *Did Mum come here? Did she look out at that view, or lean against these same standing stones? Did she look for Cowrie shells on this very beach? Watch the Sanderling startle there?*

Back in Eoligarry we sat at the long wooden table eating scrambled eggs. We heard the plane before we saw it, buzzing across the wide window-scape, listing around, veering back to the south west towards Glasgow with Kate's rolls of marbled paper somewhere in its hold. The Twin Otter's engine faded into the distance.

We spread out our maps, got out lists and notebooks and pencils, connected to the Wi-Fi. We needed to join some dots, do some route planning. It was a dance, going from map to iPod to phone to kettle, reading texts on the phone that were beginning to tip towards poetry: *Re Iochdar. Gentle accordionist Billy McPhee will give you grazing*. This house was built for stopping in, for doing nothing, for going nowhere. From the moment you sat down to take your shoes off, and read the words engraved on the bench *Where is the time for contemplation*, you had no choice but to slow down and be quiet. I loved travelling with Shuna for many reasons, but a major one was that we were both happy in silence. The long rides we'd already done together had taught us that.

The windows constantly pulled my gaze. I wanted to do route planning, but the urge to just watch and do nothing was stronger. A duck-speckle here, three kayaks there, a lilt of seaweed under the incoming tide or was it an otter, a pulse of wind, the Eriskay ferry gliding white-necked in the distance. Then a Swallow bashed into the glass. I went outside and bent over him, his tiny body stunned and panting. Our blissful view. His violence. I put him in a sunny spot out of the breeze, and half an hour later he had flown away.

The tide was high by the time we left the house. The plan was to explore some of the wing-like promontory of Eoligarry. We wanted to visit the medieval church at Kilbarr, built in memory of St Finnbarr, Chille Bharra in the Gaelic, and the dun, the Iron Age hill fort. Then we'd bring the ponies back to the house to tack up, having hopefully bought some oysters on the way. By then the tide would be low enough for us to go for an evening gallop on the Airport beach.

The medieval church was tiny and enchanting. It felt size-appropriate to Eoligarry whose only hill was 102 metres high. Primroses swamped the grass between the gravestones. Old carved stones, new polished granite stones, tiny plainsong stones leaning towards the past were decorated only with Lichens. Compton Mackenzie, author of *Whisky Galore*, was buried somewhere here. We sat and sat, listening to Skylarks singing, so high we couldn't see them. The remains of two chapels in the burial ground were bonded with shell and lime mortar, salt-chalked Barra Snails grazed on the greenery between the stones on the gable ends. These Barra Snails would have been eaten by the monks of old and were now coming back into fashion as a delicacy. Strands of blue sky were breaking through above us and it promised to be a glorious evening. A camper van and its German owners arrived and altered the perspective of everything. We smiled a hello and left quietly. It felt as if there wasn't room for the four of us. We passed a newer, bigger church, St Mary's, where smartly dressed parishioners were filing out from a Saturday meeting. Looking up at the skyline, we decided to give the dun a miss. Indolence was singing in our bones. We turned onto the track that led north to the ponies' field with Lapwings hurtling around us in loops, crying their rubber-soled squeaks. We walked as quietly as possible on and out of their world. Ross and Chief had spotted us and were standing with their heads over the gate, keen and pristine against the sea.

We led them down through a tiny gate onto the beach of Traidh Sguirabhal. I stood on a bank of marram grass and got onto Ross's warm back. His dark coat was a magnet to any heat from the sun. He took long strides between lines of empty cockle shells that had been left behind by the receding tide. The sky was reflected in the wet sand and birdsong rolled down to us from the dunes. Chief, silver-white as the clouds, shied away from the wavelets spreading rumours at his heels. It seemed both ponies were feeling good about life.

We left the beach where Eoligarry's corpulent black-stone jetty juts into the sea. I waited by the gate of 'Gerry's house' with Ross and Chief while Shuna went to knock on the door. A flurry of Rhode Island Reds clucked and ruffled in the wind and lines of bright washing flapped on the line. 'Four dozen for £24, what a bargain!' Shuna said when she came back, smiling and holding four red net bags full of Oysters. 'I got two dozen to leave for Richard too.' Back in the house I put the Oysters in the fridge, taking care to have their flat sides up. Shuna had explained that if you rest them on their curved side they are less stressed, and if they open their shells a bit they won't lose all of their juices. You can keep them like that for a week, and if they aren't eaten they can be released back into the sea. The ponies grazed in the garden while we had a cup of tea, giving the tide just a little bit longer to pull out.

We galloped and galloped and whooped and yelled at the top of our voices. Not since Australia had I had so much open ground to gallop on. Firm safe sand. The hoofbeats changed tone as we moved from dry to wet sand, through patches of sand ripples and tidal-dimples and across the finest skimming of seawater. The horses were up for it, racing head to head, skitting sideways around remnant pools and jinking in tandem at things only they could see with their peripheral horse-vision. At the far end of Airport Beach, they came to a standstill and we laughed out loud. The evening had turned truly golden, and as we waited for the ponies to stop blowing, a slide of rainbow appeared above the red-roofed house at Crannag.

We rode back towards a woman cockling on her own. She leaned a full sack against a car which ran with rust onto the sand. Her face lit up as we got closer. 'I thought I was seeing things,' she said, 'but right enough...' Her words trailed off into a grin. 'I like horses. I watch the showjumping on the TV sometimes.' She shook her head, her smile fading. 'Oh, but they put those horses through a lot.' Her empathy was deeply touching. Alongside Orosay, we watched two Oystercatchers lose a battle with a Hooded Crow that flew away with an egg poised in its wide beak, its silver mantle shining like armour. The Oystercatchers were left calling in distress while up ahead the Hoodie landed and tottered triumphantly in the ragged grass. We got off the ponies and sat on some black rocks. Clumps of Sea Thrift were on the turn, flowers just past their best but still glowing pink near their centres. I felt grounded, melded to the rock. The flush of adrenalin after the gallop had left me spent and still. I could see Richard's house across the sands, let my eyes trace the land-line back to the point, past old runrigs catching the low-flung light, past dots of Cattle, past Taigh Ciolla where Rob's mother had come during the war.

On the way back, passing the pier at Eoligarry, the tide was so far out that Gerry's oyster beds were fully exposed. Bladderwrack and Sea Lettuce draped the metal frames where the Oysters lustred pewter in their baskets. Oyster farming is non-polluting and sustainable, unlike many other methods of fish farming in Scotland. An hour later we'd be sitting looking out to where the hills of Rum were spun like gold in faraway sunshine, and a dozen Oysters would be going down smoothly with a squeeze of lemon.

Back at Rob and Kate's croft I let Ross loose and went down to the corner of the field with my bead purse. I knew which one I wanted to leave here today, it was clear glass, grooved like a cockle shell: glass, *glainne*, that purest rendering down of sand. I carefully tied it to the fence under the primrose bank. On an impulse I picked out another bead and tied it alongside.

This one was the same pearlescent baby-blue as the Sound of Barra in the falling light. A flock of Oystercatchers lifted in a kerfuffle from the sand, then settled again a little further off, all turning in the air to land facing in exactly the same direction. I took my phone out of my pocket and checked for enough signal to send a text to Martin. It wasn't until after I'd sent it that I saw predictive texting had changed Eriskay to Erudita, which sounded like a lovely place to be headed to on the third Sunday in May.

DAY FOUR

Barra to South Uist

Booked onto the 15.45 CalMac sailing between Ardmhor in the north of Barra and Eriskay, we had plenty of time to explore the chambered cairns Rob and Kate had told us about. 'Better than Stonehenge,' they'd laughed, 'but they can be hard to find.'

Armed with our map we drove back along the west road, took a right turn past Shuna's postbox and carried on up the straight township road signed 'Craigston'. We passed a house sign, '121a Craigston'. How did that work, I wondered, there were only a handful of houses we could see in this township, let alone 121?

We parked at the end of the tarmac road by a *Bird of Prey Trail* sign. *Eagles are most easily spotted as they break the skyline*, it told us, a good reminder to look up. We set off due east along the track. It was a soft grey day. Remains of houses came into relief on the hillside above us, thick curved walls splashed with lime-white lichen. The softer I kept my gaze, the more ruins I saw, lifting up out of that craggy hillside in a mute layering of rounded stones. It occurred to me that maybe '121a Craigston' had taken into account these past dwellings, a continuous totting-up through the ages as bungalows sprouted below them.

Below the track, through the iron framework of a bed-end gate, sharper lines cut into the lower slopes of this glen. Telephone poles, pebble-dashed gable ends, Sky TV dishes, wind turbines, were all signs of a more comfortable way of life. I brought my focus back to the gate, where human ingenuity was visible at a micro level. It was held together by a concoction of twenty-first century fibres: flat webbing strap, the kind you get on a sheep dosing bottle, blue polypropylene BT rope, and green flatfish netting. They were all attached to gateposts that leaned tiredly and had lichen furring the sides that faced away from the sea. There were little pockets of shelter everywhere in this windswept glen. Beside us, the circular wall of an old sheep fank was brimful of Irises with yellow flowers just beginning to open.

At the end of the track we came to a set of metal sheep pens and walked through them to an old shieling. Its walls were four feet thick, the thatched roof covering was long gone but black roofing-felt, wooden battens and chicken wire were still present, and the stones that at one time would have held the thatch down. These were tied by their middles and hung along the eaves. The door was locked. We peered through a glass-less window into the gloom where a faint algae bloom greened the concrete floor between islands of rusted cans, a lidless aluminium teapot, and the cast-iron hearth. There were three chairs, backless, relics from a village hall perhaps, their laminated ply seats glowing electric seventies blue.

I straightened up, smiling. I liked this place. I liked its cheery demise, its graceful decay. The softnesses of black Moss pushed up like velvet buttons along the roof rafters. It lifted my spirits on this grey day. I got out the bead purse. There was no question, the large marble bead belonged to this place. I threaded it onto a piece of silk and wove it firmly through the rope that was holding down the thatch stones. The bead had a cream-equator, gradating outwards into strata of greys and silvers, and lay like a bright planet against galaxies of darkening Lichens and Mosses.

Shuna and I looked at the map, then looked up the hill and pointed out imaginary lines to follow, there was no path here. We stepped over old turf dykes, through constellations of Bog Cotton, across banks of Ling Heather and Deer Grass and Black Sedge. From the nose of the hill two faces peered down at us, a ewe with white face markings showing some Swale blood, and her black-faced lamb. She lifted pale eyebrows towards us, her lamb's eyes lost in the pitch of its face. The pair blended into the monochrome of the leaning rocks. We'd found our Neolithic chambered cairn. As we approached the sheep moved off with a scrabble of hooves on boulders.

Large stones that once would have stood upright now leaned and lay in a relaxed muddle. We loved that there wasn't a path, a sign, a fence; nothing to say what this place was, nothing to keep livestock out, nothing to be precious about. I sat down, spreading my palms wide across the thin lichen-crust of what I guessed was the tomb's capstone. I closed my eyes, in no hurry to leave. Chambered cairns have long been a safe place for me, that was something I'd inherited from my mother, a love of standing stones. Her passion for ancient history was what first took Mum to Cairnholy in South West Scotland, the place I lived the longest when I was growing up, a whole seven years. I think it's also the place that has most left its mark on me.

I lived at Cairnholy from 1981 until I left home in 1988 when I was sixteen, and must have spent hundreds of hours on the burial mound. It was my refuge, this Neolithic chambered cairn, officially known as Cairnholy II. From there the land sloped downhill towards the jagged outline of the standing stones at Cairnholy I, and beyond that to the Solway Firth. In the opposite direction rose Cairnholy Hill. At its base were flat rocks indented with eroded cup and ring markings. Above them the slopes lifted into the hill proper, its contours weighted with stone dykes, its face scored with the precise lines of sheep tracks through heather and bracken.

If it was raining, I'd crawl into the burial chamber with a book to be sheltered by the capstone. It looked precarious, the stone balancing there on three points, but it had stayed in place for over four thousand years. I felt safe there. The grass at Cairnholy was cut by Historic Scotland. The gate's hinges were oiled, its wood given a fresh coat of Butinox every year. The dykes around the mound were well maintained. The 'mowdy man' came and dropped poisoned worms into the mole hills. It was a manicured place and there was signage, all of which I found reassuring. You knew where you were. Next to the mound was a pebble-dashed bungalow where Burt, the shepherd, lived with his family. There was gravel in his driveway and frosted glass on the bathroom windows, and behind those was Cairnholy Farmhouse, our home. There was no gravel outside our house, only bedrock. Stone steps, depressed in the middle, led down to the rough granite walls of the house. There was a door on the right into a coal shed, and straight ahead was the back door into the scullery. We only ever used the back door. Once inside you pressed a thumb-worn latch on the door on the right to enter the kitchen which is where life unfolded.

It was wood-lined halfway up the walls, and where the wood met the plaster there was a tiny shelf. All around the room, on this shelf, were Mum's treasures: a dead Stag Beetle, a dried-out Frog, Fish fossils, a carved wooden figure, the size of a bantam's egg, that when you tilted it forwards its eyes and tongue popped out on tiny ivory stalks. The kitchen was the warmest and best lit room in the house. In the early days the room was dominated by Tilley lamps that hissed and spluttered, and a rust-edged gas heater that sent out waves of damp warmth. Once the Esse was installed the gas heater moved outside to Mum's jewellery workshop where its fumes intoxicated the tiny insects that lived in the wool-lined walls. They dropped by their hundreds onto her bead tray, or sizzled microscopically on the red-hot tip of her welder.

We all became slaves to the Esse. Wood collecting, wood chopping, wood carrying, and when wood was scarce there were coal and anthracite deliveries that gobbled the overdraft facility. Paul was the main labourer though. He'd leave his book-designing desk to go out into the coal shed and fill the scuttle. He'd riddle the stove feverishly until his glasses steamed up. His knuckles, red from the cold in his office, would become dusted with black and he'd have to scrub his hands before going back to the pristine pages of the latest manuscript from André Deutsch. A short time later he'd be back, and riddle again, until the air flowed and the fire burned hot ready for dinner time. Paul did all of the cooking. Most nights we had baked potatoes, onions fried with curry powder and canned tuna fish added at the end, a salad of iceberg lettuce. It was my job to make the salad dressing: two thirds sunflower oil, one third white wine vinegar, pinch of Colman's mustard powder, salt and pepper, and 'Bob's your uncle', as Paul used to say.

We'd eat meals listening to Radio 4. The 7 O'Clock News, The Archers and Front Row would usually coincide with dinner time. We heard all about the miners' strikes.

'You can thank your bloody father, he voted for that witch,' said Mum.

Apparently, my dad was to blame for a lot of things other

49

than the pit closures. He was to blame for the teachers' strikes, for us not being taught Latin at school, and for us not being able to swim in the Solway Firth because of the radioactive waste from Sellafield. It was also, according to Mum, his fault that we were poor. She was constantly fighting him for more child maintenance. Sitting on Barra, my hands on the ancient stones, memory after memory was being upturned.

I'm sitting on a stool with Paul's spittle landing on my face and he's screaming at me: 'Your father is a fucking cretin,' over and over again. His face is getting redder, his lips wetter, his glasses flash. 'Do you FUCKING understand?'

I must have broken down in the end or wouldn't have been allowed off the stool, but I don't remember. I've blocked it from my memory. I don't remember Mum ever stepping in for me with Paul. I'd stand up for her and face the consequences, but that was when I still would have done anything for her. It felt to me like I got the brunt of Paul's wrath. Tom had fishing in common with him, a passion that bonded them, and by then my older brother Will was living with Dad, which had happened quickly after Paul came on the scene.

Paul loved fishing. He and my uncle, Mum's brother Robin, would spend days and nights on the Skyreburn and the Palnure. They'd come home late and sit at the table, their catch laid out in front of them. Robin and Paul would weigh the fish, gut them, examine the contents of their stomachs, discuss their markings, their age, sex, the pool they were caught in, the height of the water. With dirt-engrained fingers they'd open the jaws, feel the teeth, fan out the fins. This ritual would go on for hours while joints were smoked and pots of tea were drunk.

Paul took care of us. He got us up in the mornings with his nakedness hanging. I hated that. He'd shout up the stairs at us, *come on, kiddos*. He'd make sure we were getting out of bed, doubly tough in the winter when ice crystals had grown overnight on the duvets. He'd have toast ready on the table, and insist that we ate breakfast. He'd make us wear our coats and I hated that too, but it was a mile-and-a-half walk to the bus in all weathers.

Burt, the shepherd, would give us a lift if he passed us. Burt was softly-spoken and drove a pickup that started every time, and his sheepdogs wagged their tails at us. Tom and I would take it in turns to help him at lambing time. He taught us how to lamb ewes, and how to skin a dead lamb so it could be used to twin on another lamb. How to encourage a weak lamb to have its first suck. Sometimes he'd have us in for tea. In Burt's house they ate oven chips and had central heating and fitted carpets. They always had chocolate biscuits in the tin, and they had a TV. Mum said Burt was a peasant on account of him wanting to cut down the Rowan tree in the sheep fank. I suspect it was on account of lots of other things too, pebble dash and teabags, for example.

Not being common was important to Mum. So was being interesting.

'Why do you stay with Paul, Mum?'

'Because he's interesting, darling.'

She loved that he'd been a professional musician, a founding member of a band called The Third Ear Band. He'd rubbed shoulders with famous artists, made albums and played in Roman Polanski's film, *Macbeth*. She loved that his music was avant-garde. He'd play his oboe for hours, music that made your jaw and knees tighten, and would come back into the kitchen with huge dark patches under his arms. His piano playing was easier to listen to, like having Radio 3 on. Sometimes I'd stop and listen in wonder at the music coming from the sitting room. The rest of us hardly ever went in there because it was too cold, but on Christmas Day we'd light the fire and go in and listen to records. Paul had hundreds and, sometimes, when the house was empty, I'd go in and play them. I remember the first time I heard David Bowie's *Aladdin Sane*. By the time the stylus had vibrated its way to the end of 'Time' I knew I'd passed through a threshold of no return.

I lived at Cairnholy for seven years, the amount of time your body needs to renew every single cell. In those seven years I spent a lot of time reading in a Neolithic burial chamber. I spent a lot of time walking in the fields, on the hill and down by the burn. I touched stones wherever I found them, smooth round damp ones in the burn, jagged dry ones in the dyke. To this day, the feel of a stone in my palm soothes me. I touched the trees too, especially the Rowans polished satin-smooth by Belted Galloway Cattle rubbing against them. If it was warm I'd press my face against the bark, inhaling smells lifted by the sun: sweetness of sap, muskiness of cow. In those seven years I had my first sexual feelings when my pony's whiskers brushed against my neck. I grew up alongside my younger brother and fell in love with his best friend. I dreamed hard. I studied hard and when I was sixteen I left.

By then Mum had been diagnosed with a brain tumour. We'd heard her having epileptic fits in her loft bedroom above the kitchen. Blood-chilling wails, like the sound of a rabbit screaming in the fixed glare of a stoat. Eerie. Inhuman. It was all my fault apparently, so Paul said. Best for everybody, really, if I left, and in the end I really wanted to go. There was no reason to stay, so it seemed. Post-brain surgery must have been a terrible time for Mum but, in the midst of all that turmoil, I left, carrying hurt and defensiveness that would never dissolve enough.

The last time I was back at Cairnholy was for Paul's funeral in 1997. He had hanged himself in the barn where Mum found him with 'a peaceful expression on his face'. She was still living with him, but the marriage was over. The animals had all died: the horses, the cat, the dog. Paul had nursed Mum through cancer, squeezed lemons and oranges for her in their thousands, learnt to drive and, after all that, had wanted a divorce. Suffering from depression he was prescribed anti-depressants that were later linked to suicide. By the time he hanged himself Mum was already involved with someone else. She had, apparently, finally stopped being interested in Paul's 'interesting'. By then he'd taken to wearing his boxer shorts over the top of his jeans, and was surviving solely on sardines and brown rice.

Mum glammed up for the cremation by putting her make-up on the way he had liked. In-your-face emerald green eye shadow and thick sweeping eyeliner. She had his own music playing. The Third Ear Band, with the lyrics *and the curtain draws across* sounding as the curtains closed around the coffin. It occurred to me that it was fitting, really, that Paul should go into the flames after so many years of shovelling fuel into the Esse, but I was shocked at the force of my grief. That was the day Mum had giggled and giggled, but I understand her giggles better now. There was so much about her that I understood better now. Two weeks later I lost the baby I was carrying. Later, much later, I wondered if it had been for the best. The baby would have absorbed my shock, and it wouldn't have been great to have carried such memories in its cells. I doubt I'd be able to say that if I hadn't gone on to have three gorgeous healthy children.

A movement up the hill caught my eye, the Ewe and Lamb were still up there, biding their time until I left. The Ewe was alert. She bent her muzzle around and checked in with her Lamb. I stood up, straightening my stiffening knees, wiping my tears. I looked around for Shuna, who had set off across the hill and was now small in the distance, heading towards the other archaeological site marked on the map, 'Dun-Bharpa'.

I got out the bead purse again. I was feeling raw, part of me wanted to leave all the beads here and be done with it. Mum's presence was so strong, maybe I could leave her and my memories here. Just like that. I imagined pouring the rest of the beads over the stones, into the caved-in entrances to the tomb chambers. But I knew I couldn't. I needed to make this journey through the Hebrides with her, to be with her, bead by bead. I took out a tiny, asymmetric piece of amber that glowed like an ember and pressed it into a fold in the large upright stone near me. It was held precisely, gently, in the flank of that rock. It burned brightly in the water-laden air, and would perhaps burn brightly there way beyond my lifetime.

Then I picked out a small black pearl and laid it on the capstone I'd been sitting on. It shone too, but darkly, like a bear's eye inside a cave. The wind or a rubbing sheep might move it sometime soon, so I picked it up and bent to place it inside the tomb. I withdrew quickly, my forearm welting with the fierce bite of a stinging nettle. I had been warned. I placed the pearl back on the horizontal slab, let the Sheep or the wind or the Faeries have it then. I set off to join Shuna.

We traversed the hill back down towards the pickup. The tops of old dykes, the rest of them long since sunk, lay across the boggy slopes like strings of pearls. I stopped beside an old Massey Ferguson like the one Martin does most of the farm work on at home. A 1964 model, it is the same age as him. Just the wheel rims of this Barra tractor were visible, and its red-rusted engine, and the aluminium clutch housing gone chalky with age. A trailer was still attached, its struts visible, the wooden boards mossed over. It had come a cropper who knows how long ago and I wondered what else was buried under this shifting time-steeped hillside.

Back near the car I slowed my steps. A small grey Eriskay mare was standing ahead of us. I have a sweet spot for Eriskays.

I have one at home and am full of admiration for this feisty breed which at one time was a mainstay of life in these islands, carrying seaweed and peats and people. The Mare was standing in the lee of a white container, one of those transport containers that are recycled all over the Highlands and Islands as workshops, feed stores, field shelters. I hadn't seen the Mare on the way up, she must have been out of sight at the gable end. The ground was poached around the container and there was evidence of old hay. It looked like this was where she'd spent the winter. No sign of another pony, just some sheep further up the hillside. I looked at her, she looked back. She was sway-backed, ribby and probably very old. I wondered how long she'd been on her own. How long it had been since her companions died, or were sold? Had she ever had companions in the decades since running with her mother? I wondered if she'd been born on Eriskay and brought here. Turning away I kept on walking but my footsteps were dull, my legs hollow. It's never easy seeing a horse on its own.

'Hello, Shuna, how are you?' The man's voice was soft, west coast. Shuna's face lit up. 'Cubby! What are you doing here?'

'Beady, this is Cubby, he used to live in Kilmelford.'

His handshake was warm. We were leaning against the railings, our backs to a biting-cold wind while we kept an eye on the ponies in the trailer on the car-deck below.

'This is Anne,' he introduced us to the fresh-faced woman standing beside him. Shuna and Cubby got to catching up. With their heads close together, and the wind snatching their words, it was hard to hear them,

'Sorry, I didn't quite catch your name. Is it Biddy?' Anne asked.

'It's Beady, as in a string of beads. My real name is Leonie, but most people call me Beady.'

'How did you get Beady from Leonie?'

'My mum called me Beady when I was a baby. Beady eyes.' A familiar look of confusion passed across Anne's face. I added, 'It wasn't a bad thing. Mum loved beads. She said my eyes were shiny like beads.'

It turned out Anne was an archaeologist, and a font of knowledge about the ancient history of the Uists. She and Cubby had lived here together for a couple of years now, but she'd been coming for years before that. She was in love with both the archaeology and the music of the Uists. Place names rolled off her tongue with quiet assurance. She said to get in touch anytime if we needed more information, and by the time we docked at Eriskay my imagination was spinning with aisled houses, wheelhouses, standing stones, barps, long cairns, cup and ring markings.

During the forty-minute crossing the wind had steadily been getting stronger, and now, back in the pickup, the rain came on in a heavy burst, a proper thunder-plump. With windscreen wipers thrashing and the heater on full blast we drove off MV Loch Bhrusda and up the long steep hill away from the pier.

'Look at that?' I said, pointing below. The ragged coastline glowed with an aura of turquoise sea. Through the rain there were splashes of colour: a red roof here, a scattering of day-glo pink fishing buoys there. I recognised a green shed from the last time I was here. Martin and the children and I had come across from Barra with our bicycles for the day. We'd climbed to the summit of Beinn Sciathan where the water bottle had blown away. It had been another windy day but the views across the causeway to South Uist had been crystal clear. We'd swum and our sun-and-wind burn had stung for the rest of the day.

'We're looking for Garrynamonie Church on the right,' said Shuna. 'Morag says we can't miss it, it's a big grey building where her croft is. She sounds really keen to meet the ponies.'

'That must be the church,' I said. It looked like a super-sized military bunker but for the cross on top. We pulled in beside it. The engine died and, parked in the shadow of that building, the rain lashing the window, my spirits dropped.

'Quite weird,' Shuna said simply.

We pulled on our waterproofs and stepped outside. The rain eased just as a small silver car pulled up. Morag came up to us, all smiles and exuding good health. Her skin was tanned and her hazelnut-brown eyes were luminous. She was full of delight at the ponies. We moved away from the church towards a roof-less low stone building. One gable end was gone.

'This is my croft house,' she said, her pride lighting up the dreich afternoon. She showed us around, pointing things out: the reach of raised ground where she thought the remains of a Neolithic long cairn were: the march boundary between her croft and the common grazing: a patch of boggy ground that she hoped the ponies would know to stay away from. Months later I'd learn that two possible meanings for Garrynamonie are 'garden of the moorland', or 'the wall that separates the peat bog'.

Morag dragged an old bath to a tap, saying it was a good water supply. As the bath filled with clear water, she told us stories about the croft and her ancestors, but I wanted to know about the church. My eyes kept being drawn back to it and I thought it even uglier from this angle. In the end I just pointed at it and lifted my eyebrows. 'Our Lady of Sorrows, the brutalist Roman Catholic Church.' Morag laughed. 'You know, a lot of people really love it, I'm told. It's a famous modernist building, Category B listed. It's got a cross that lights up at night and guides sailors out at sea.'

'But it's so close to your house, and right between you and your view of the sea.'

'Aye, well, they got hold of the site while my great uncle was away serving in WWI, and some joukery-pawkery that was.' I wanted to hear more, but we needed to get the ponies settled and put up the tent. Morag left us to it, saying how much she enjoyed seeing animals on the croft and that she was hoping to get some sheep this summer. She wished us well on our journey and sprang away across the rough ground towards Easabhal. 'An incredible hill for views,' she'd said, shrugging on a backpack. I hoped we'd see her again.

We'd stopped off earlier and booked a table at the Polochar Inn. There had been a football game playing on the wall-mounted screen in the corner of the bar, and the room had smelt of woodsmoke and Duck toilet cleaner and old beer. The place had been empty, apart from three men and a woman standing at the bar watching the game. The woman had been drinking a pint of Guinness, tapping her Crocs in time with 'Parachutes' by Coldplay. A few hours later, the place was buzzing and we realised how lucky we'd been to get a table. We were soon buoyed by delicious food and the swell of laughter and chat all around us. It felt like we were the only diners not speaking Gaelic there that night.

'There's a text from Morag,' Shuna said, wiping rain off her face as we returned to the pickup. 'She's invited us to camp on her floor if we want.' If we'd been cold in the tent the other night at Tangasdale I dreaded to think what it would be like in this weather.

'Yes, please!' I answered. We drove back towards the lit-up cross high on the roof of 'Our Lady of Sorrows', slowing to check the ponies as they sheltered in the lee of the croft house. Shuna passed me her phone so I could read out Morag's directions.

'Keep going to Daliburgh, turn right past the office supplies store, I'm just past white fire station on way to Lochboisdale, you'll see the car...'

A milky-skinned statue of Jesus lifted out of the gloom on our right. We were both feeling blessed as the wind buffeted the pickup and Jesus sank back into the darkness.

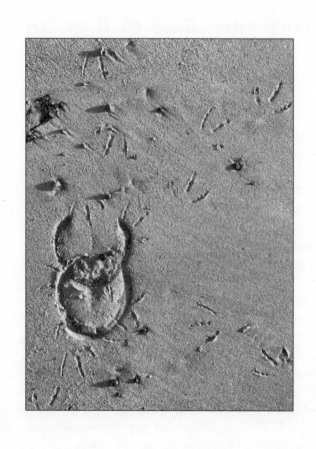

DAY FIVE

Garrynamonie to Bowmore

Rain squalls spluttered against the west-facing windows as we packed our sleeping mats. Wind pushed under the sills. Morag's house was spartan, bare floorboards, bare walls. Everything was pleasingly minimal. Yet on the mantelpiece a string of little fairy lights twinkled in the low daylight, and amongst them rested a postcard of Kevin MacNeil's poem in Gaelic and English words. *Seahorses*. I picked it up.

> *I dreamt I was the seafloor and you were the weight*
> *of the ocean pressing down on me*
> *your quiet words of love in my ears now and again*
> *golden, elegant and strange, like seahorses*
> *like grace-notes, tiny floating saxophones.*

Morag was sitting at her desk by the window, tap-tapping on her laptop. 'Sorry,' she said, 'I have to get something off to the Scottish Land Court this morning.' She'd been telling us the night before about the case she was preparing to take to the Scottish Land Court to ensure no more of her croft was appropriated. 'I just have to do this, this wee piece of land, well, it means the world to me.'

As well as safeguarding the boundary of her croft she was also trying to resolve a 'machair share'. Machair is the more fertile, arable, low-lying coastal land by the sea where crops are grown for feed and animals are often grazed in winter. Morag said that many records show that a machair share exists but that it was taken while a widow occupied the croft. She talked at speed about the Land Records Agency, Highland Archives, archives of the Scottish Land Court, formerly known as the Crofters Commission, the National Archives of Scotland on Prince's Street in Edinburgh, and the Land Registry of Scotland. She talked about land parcels, landowner records, the Freedom of Information Act, heritable tenures, the 1886 Crofting Act, national maps at Sighthill in Edinburgh. Her knowledge was immense.

When she was working 'off-island' she took every opportunity to research her case. She spoke warmly of the amazing number of people out there who were willing to give her 'a wee steer'. She exuded intelligence and courage and, as she spoke, a salt-burned willow thrashed against the window next to her.

Shuna and I went through to the kitchen to make coffee. Next to the light switch was a yellow heart-shaped Post-it note: 'I am independent of the good opinion of others.' Tears prickled behind my eyes. Morag had talked to us about 'visibility in a small community, and the church', she'd told us how since her case was notified in the local papers she'd got a new mobile phone, was locking her front door and had come off social media. I was in awe of her determination to see this through and see justice done for herself and her ancestors. As she typed, Shuna and I ate porridge, charged our phones and repacked the saddlebags. We pottered and chatted happily, not in any hurry to go out into that grey gale-force day. I picked up a stone from the windowsill, iridescent in hues of blues and greens. 'That's labradorite,' Morag said. 'They say it's a master healing stone.

It raises consciousness and dispels illusions. It's a crystal to help combine logic and insight.'

We sat in the horse trailer having a second breakfast of hard-boiled eggs and Tabasco while listening to the rain blasting against the metal sides.

'We'd better get going,' Shuna said, 'doesn't look like this rain is going to stop anytime soon.' As we tacked up I noticed Chief was shivering, his haunches and flanks quivering as the rain fell off him in runnels. The ponies needed to move. We locked the pickup and set off down the township road towards the sea, lowering our heads into the wind and walking in silence. I was thinking of Morag's courage. She reminded me of Mum, she'd been brave like that too, with a fierce fighting spirit, and would stand up for what she thought was right. She had seemed to not give a damn about others' opinions. Except when it came to men maybe. With certain men she'd had a blind spot. Otherwise, when love or sex wasn't in the equation, she was fearless.

Mum and I were so different in that way. I'd always been frightened of upsetting the applecart. I like to keep the peace. I was working on changing that though, of not being so affected by others' opinions. Having realised that I was getting more like her as I got older, I was finally accepting that we had a lot in common. It was she who passed to me this love of horses. This lifelong passion that has been my bedrock, but where she would go fox hunting on borrowed horses, or gallop with Gypsies in the South of France, I tended to play it safe. I wasn't brave like she had been, but I was wholehearted. The etymological roots of the word 'courage' translate as wholehearted, so maybe, I was courageous too. Just in a different way.

For as long as I could remember, I'd wanted to go on a long ride, but didn't manage until I was in my thirties. This was now my fifth extended trip with horses, and by far the longest. During the Cairnholy years Mum and I had planned to do a camp ride together, but it had never materialised. I understood now how tiring life had been for her, motherhood, earning a living as an artist, maintaining a marriage. Just keeping warm had been hard. Also, who knows how long her body had been fighting a tumour before we realised she was ill. The camping trip never happened, but she had laid the foundation for my lifelong love of horses, making sure I had riding lessons when I was little, even when she was going through a divorce and had no money. Later she organised ponies for me to have on loan. First there was Puzzle, then Fury, then Mr Jones. After Mr Jones Dad bought Skye Boy for me. We really couldn't afford to keep a pony, but together they made it happen. Despite the cars being on their last legs, endless meetings with bank managers to extend the overdraft, and borrowing money from her parents for hay bills, I'd had ponies for a large part of my childhood, and for that privilege I will be eternally grateful.

When I was twelve Skipper came into our lives, a Thoroughbred cross who was the realisation of Mum's lifelong dream to have a horse of her own. He was bay with a russet muzzle, the colours of the Skipper butterfly she renamed him after. There were a few years when we rode together regularly, but it became increasingly harder to get her out. I can remember cajoling her by promising to do all the grooming and tacking up. In hindsight I'm sure the cancer must have begun to exhaust her long before it was diagnosed. With the pony years, she gave me something that has been a resource through my whole life. After I left home we would never ride together again.

When she died she left a small amount of money. Rather than doing the sensible thing and paying it into the mortgage or overdraft I bought a big bay Spanish horse, 'Jareta Principe', otherwise known as 'Gorgeous George'. His mother had been a gift from King Juan Carlos of Spain to King Hussein of Jordan. He was very 'well bred', strong, beautiful, intelligent and opinionated, Mum would definitely have approved. After she died I found amongst her books: *My Dancing White Horses, The Autobiography of Alois Podhaisky*, former chief rider at the Spanish Riding School and instrumental in rescuing the Lipizzaner stallions from Russian occupation in 1945. A famous quote of his is, 'nature can exist without art, but art can never exist without nature'. Inscribed at the front of the book is '*March 19th 1967. To Kathryn with love, Max xx*'. It was my father's present to Mum on her seventeenth birthday. They were both still at school, in love, and unaware of what was to come: the teenage pregnancy, the hurried wedding, three children and a lot of heartache. Throughout it all a mutual love and fascination with nature endured, and they were both committed to passing that passion on to their children.

Here in South Uist the ponies' hooves made a pleasing hollow sound on the wet tarmac. Down through the decades I could hear Mum's voice saying *Bombalina*, a name she reserved for me in our private moments together, and in her letters. Walking down that township road in the heavy rain I knew that I'd had her love. I'd just chosen to turn away from it for reasons that were well-founded at the time, but that no longer served me.

The ponies continued walking, bending their necks away from the driving rain and skirting around the silver puddles. Their coronet bands were soaked and shone moon-white above their black hooves. We passed a sprinkling of buildings: a stone cottage with an aquamarine-streaked tin roof, a concrete byre with no roof, bungalows set dismally to the wet wind, a thatched cottage dark with rain, parked outside it a long wheel base Transit van, its white panels smeared with rust, its doors and wheels long gone. The red shock of three gas bottles against a stone shed. In the doorway, under a low stone lintel, was a short man holding an axe. He shot us a shy, toothless smile as we passed, his eyes keenly following the ponies. The fields were fenced into a craziness of tiny triangles, a few sheep in each one. One of them stared at us, chewing in clockwise circles, showing us her single tooth. On the mainland she would have been sold long ago but here, on this sweet machair grazing, things were different. And how green the grass was. It was different out here with all that sky, even when it was overcast the light made so much more of the colours.

At the end of the tarmac road the wind was full of the tang of the sea. A wooden arrow indicated the *Machair Way*, a path that wound alongside twenty uninterrupted miles of sandy beach. We stopped to read a sign set down low.

MACHAIR LIFE+. Machair is the Gaelic term for a distinct type of coastal grassland that supports a huge diversity of plants, birds and invertebrates, some of which are now rare in the UK. Seventy per cent of the world's machair occurs in Western Scotland and is currently under threat. The MACHAIR LIFE+ Project is part funded by the LIFE+ programme of the European Union. The project aims to encourage traditional forms of crofting, a wildlife-friendly method of working the land, resulting in the creation, protection and enhancement of this unique ecosystem.

Beside the text was a line-drawing of a Corncake, the birds which, after reading Kathleen Jamie's essay *Crex-Crex*, I will forever see as 'the little Gods of the field'. I felt a familiar wave of worry, wondering what the future held for the Corncrake, and the Lapwing and the Great Yellow Bumble Bee.

As we rode northwards thick cloud glowered over a jade sea. To our right the machair shares ran in parallel lines towards the hills in the east. Some had been planted with potatoes, the sandy ridges running in concentric curved lines. Other were ploughed and swept smooth by the wind, ready to be planted. Some were already greening up, perhaps with a crop of grass and corn, a preferred choice out here for silage which would feed the cattle through the winter months. Some areas were uncultivated. The information board had talked about rotational cropping, when the ground was left fallow for two or three years, enabling breeding birds and insects to thrive amongst the wildflowers. Great rusty spheres lay amongst the dunes, iron fishing buoys washed up in storms. They grounded the landscape, weighting down its hemlines against all that airborne and seaborne transience.

We passed a green-domed tidal island, another 'Orosay'. The remains of a jetty, with just the upright timbers remaining, scored its shoreline. On our side of the tidal strand, was 'Orosay Net Station'. So said the sign attached to the fence that ringed it, ten feet tall with concrete pillars and crowned in barbed wire. On the other side of the fence were mounds of nets. Not so long ago they used to repair nets here for fish-farm cages, but now the nets were rotting away. Rows of black silage bales muscled up along the edge of industrial-looking sheds. On our side of the fence were stacks of parlour creels, the type used for Crab and Lobster fishing. They were filled with small buoys coloured in sea-faded pinks and creams and yellows. More old nets were layered like *breton crêpes* with four-foot-high rusted anchors holding them down. Everything here was taking the wind into account. Were those fierce fences for the wind too, or was something else going on in the net station?

It felt like worlds were colliding here. The delicacy of old nets and wooden built jetties with the harshness of barbed wire and concrete. Again, the scales were all out of kilter, like the church and croft house at Garrynamonie. It left me feeling uneasy as the wind supped at my breath and ribbons of silage plastic yapped in the fence wire.

Sand skittered across the beach in front of us, making Chief startle. I felt motion sick with so much shifting sand and sky. Looking out to sea to balance myself I saw a skerry of rocks draped with the black shapes of seals. They were common seals judging by the way their noses and tails scooped up at each end, like little dugout canoes. As we rode closer, they slipped one by one into the water, their heads bobbing between us and the rocks. I started to count but gave up after twenty. In an instant, sunshine switched the sea from jade to turquoise. The seals' black muzzles faced us, glistening now. They were fascinated, moving alongside us in the waves. Every now and again they'd all go under with a splash, then the sea bounced them up again like rubber balls. They looked at each other, in the same way that Ross and Chief do when they're playing, tossing their heads. As we got closer to the tideline, the seals were emboldened and moved in towards us. The ponies were wary of the waves but intrigued by the seals. We persuaded them to walk in the deeper water where it wasn't so splashy and were quickly encircled. We were infused with a sense of these exquisite creatures with their lambent eyes and long wet whiskers. Sanderling flurried ahead of us, their wings like beaten-light on the water.

Back on the dry beach we broke into a trot and the ponies' strides lengthened across the sand. The bob of seals kept pace and sunlight splashed down between the clouds. We rounded the next point breathless and laughing and the world suddenly changed. We'd left smooth sand and Sanderling and Seals behind and entered a place where Ravens stalked stiff-legged amongst thickly laid banks of rotting seaweed. Herring Gulls squabbled through yellow hooked beaks. Old silage bales lay slumped on the beach where they'd been dumped. A rain squall hit us hard and we were soaked in seconds, the wind pushing the rain through our waterproofs. The seaweed was hard going underfoot and heaved up the smell of rotting cabbage. We were glad when we were on the Marram Grass again, breathing in lungfuls of turfy air, and rejoined the Machair Way that curved along behind the dunes. Pink Pigeons lifted off ploughed earth.

'Fancy some lunch?' I pointed to a shed up ahead. We stepped out of the wind into the semi-darkness of the cattle shelter. The roof was low and flat and rain pinged overhead. The building was relatively new, judging by the small amount of rust on the box-profile sheeting, and had the sweet herbal smell of dry cow dung. After leaving school I went to Australia and worked as a jillaroo on a cattle station in Queensland for six months, and that smell reminds me of sunshine and space and galloping horses. I loved that spell in my life, not that I was particularly happy in myself, but it was a huge adventure, and it was good to be away from everything at home. Dad phoned looking for me. Weeks had gone by and they hadn't heard. As a parent I can now appreciate how worrying that must have been, but at the time, with no mobile phones, no Facebook, no emails, I hadn't given it much thought. I was too busy living in the moment. Sweaty dusty adventures hurtling through hilly scrubland after long-legged Brahman Cattle.

I remember getting a letter from Mum, the envelope addressed in her familiar left-handed writing, rounded and jaggy at the same time. I don't recall the details, just the way I felt after reading it: wracked with guilt, confusion, rage, helplessness. Sitting in the Toyota Ute with Kay, the manager, on our way to repair fences. The look of incomprehension on her face as I sobbed and sobbed. I couldn't explain to her, I couldn't put into words that which I had no way of understanding myself, but I see in that scene how messed up I was around Mum. There was love undeniably, but there was also sadness, dislike, mistrust and a lot of confusion.

Shuna and I ate smoked mussels and oatcakes for lunch. We made tea and passed the cup backwards and forwards to each other. It was good to be out of the wind, so we leant back against the walls. The ponies were happy to rest, standing quietly tied to the wooden frame of the shed. The wind had taken it out of us all. There was a single dove-grey Rabbit's foot on the ground near me. I picked up a handful of the dry dung and crumbled it between my fingers. Even in full waterproofs, with rain hammering overhead and wind finding every nail-hole to squeeze through, the smell pulled me back to Australia. Lunchtimes when the Horses would be tied to Eucalyptus trees and we would open our leather saddlebags, reaching in for the sandwiches we'd carefully wrapped in newspaper that morning. Always beef sandwiches. Beef for breakfast, lunch and dinner. I stretched my hand out to touch the telegraph pole. It was shiny where Cattle had rubbed against it and my heart felt full of sunshine. After twenty-seven years those neural pathways were still in good health.

Ross and Chief lifted their heads and started to shift their weight between hooves. We gave them an oatcake each, packed up, and set off stiffly into the wind; we'd got chilled sitting down for so long in our damp clothes. Shuna looked at the map. 'We're north of Daliburgh now, Angus McPhee will have ridden this stretch on his way to war. Did you ever get round to reading *The Silent Weaver*?'

I shook my head. 'I will though.'

'In the first chapter he's riding down here, before heading across to Lochboisdale to get the boat. It makes the hairs on the back of your neck stand up. There's a photograph of Angus and his fine gelding. That's what it says, his fine gelding...' She fell silent.

It would be months before I finally got round to reading it, sitting in my writing box on a diluvial November afternoon, 3pm and almost dark, my tears blurring the broken arms of winter-bracken outside the window.

Early in September 1939, riders in battledress cantered down a broad, grassy plain on the western edge of Europe. The young men of Uist were going to war again. (...) They and their animals were the last representatives of an equestrian culture which had flourished on the greensward of western Uist for millennia.

As they rode to war they skirted mile after mile of ground which their people had turned over for grains and root vegetables using horse-drawn ploughs. They passed over the arenas for popular horse races in the nineteenth and twentieth centuries. They led their mounts through communities which had not yet been colonised by the motor car, the lorry and the tractor.

They rode from all parts of the three distinct islands of North Uist, Benbecula and South Uist. Some districts contributed more horse soldiers than others, by virtue of their greater reliance on horses in everyday crofting life and consequently their superior horsemanship.

One such district was Iochdar at the north end of South Uist. "The horses in Iochdar were famous throughout the Uists," said a local priest. "The Iochdar people have always had the reputation of being 'big farmers' and the horses were the most important farm animals. They had to be fed first – every type of croft or farm work depended on them."

The young Lovat Scouts who rode out of Iochdar on 4 September 1939 included a tall, shy, quietly spoken 24-year-old named Angus Joseph McPhee. (...)

Angus and his comrades ignored the main arterial road which ran through the middle of the long island of South Uist. Instead they took their horses, invariably their best and favourite horses, southwards down the machair, along that broad, grassy, westernmost plain, with the Atlantic Ocean surging on their right and the high brown hills of Uist rising on their left, for almost 20 miles until they turned east to the ferry port of Lochboisdale.

Angus McPhee and the other Lovat Scouts from Iochdar rode proud and erect, in their tunics and their Balmoral bonnets with a diced band, through the busy, familiar townships of the machair. They were almost the only ordinary soldiers from Britain to take their horses to the second industrial European war of the twentieth century. They were amongst the very last active, rather than ceremonial, British horse soldiers. They were also the only members of the British Army whose horses' bridles were traditionally hand-plaited from coastal marram grass.

Months before we left on the trip Shuna had told me how Angus McPhee had gone off to war, come back damaged, and been sent to Craig Dunain, a psychiatric hospital near Inverness. He'd stayed there for fifty years, not speaking, but making things by weaving wild flowers, grass, leaves, and sheep's wool. He'd eventually returned to his beloved Uist in his eighties. Shuna had got in touch with Pip Weaser, a basket-maker who lives locally to her, to ask about making us bridles from marram grass. It was a lovely idea that never quite got off the ground, but sometimes the thought is enough, living on in our imaginations as a notion, or, like the growing list of places we wouldn't manage to visit on this trip, it can be stored away for another day.

We rode for miles, alternating between the beach and the dunes, the afternoon brightening all the time. The track switched between farm vehicle tracks and narrower paths shared by walkers and sheep, rabbits and cattle. The sun easing into the west balanced the clouds. The hills of Barra were behind us, and to our right South Uist opened up in layers: cultivated machair, then a strip of grass sward with faraway Cattle silhouetted against silver lochs, and beyond that the Heather hills still brown from winter. The sun roamed across the landscape spotlighting a single silver Swan, a red Calf, the gold-gilt of Marram Grass. Our shadows were stretching out long to the east when we moved inland from the shore. We passed a single standing stone, a toggle on the Buttercup-felted machair. In front of Loch Toronais, the ground changed underfoot.

'Oh my God,' I breathed, 'look at those flowers, they go for miles.' I jumped off Ross and squatted down.

'They're Pansies, the tiniest I've ever seen.' They were flame-yellow with crimson rays across their petals. Droves of Daisies too, their petals closing for the night over yolk-yellow centres. 'Can you hold Ross for a moment?' I said, passing the reins up to Shuna. I needed to see the world through flower-eyes. A myriad of bright Pansy-faces watched me as I lay down in their terrain of laughter and light. When I stood up, I stepped into Ross's shadow. It was woven of dusk and daisy-stars. *His shadow, his soul*, I thought, as Shuna handed me my reins. Back in the saddle my eyelashes were wet, my heart strung tight.

Beyond Loch Toronais a fence separated us from a rake of machinery: heavy field rollers, harrows, big tractors with their spikes to the sky, round-bale feeders, water containers all neatly lined up and ready to do whatever was necessary. Ahead of us a Cow was scratching her white face against a gate. We were following the Hebridean Way now, a new walking route which had absorbed the older Machair Way, and a circular sign nailed to the fence clearly indicated that the way on was through this gate. There were scores of cows and calves grazing on grassy flats that seemed to stretch as far as the walls of Ormacleit Castle far in the distance. We have a herd of Luings at home. I feel comfortable around cows, and Ross does too. He's used to them. Nonetheless, I have a healthy respect for cows I don't know, especially when they have young calves at foot, and these were big continental crosses with the muscled stamp of Simmental and Limousin. They were a magnificent bunch, rippling with good health, and there was nothing for it but to ride through them. I got off to open the gate and the Cow backed away. A nick in her ear showed where she'd lost a tag. She was so close I could smell her, and wanted to reach out and touch the damp swirls where a friend had been licking her. The ponies were on their toes with cow excitement. The rest of the herd eyed us up but made no signs of coming towards us. For now they were content to stay where they were, enjoying the warmth of the afternoon.

The gatepost was today's bead place. It was made from the trunk of a big tree, some kind of pine. It was weathered silver and weeds had seeded themselves on top. I chose another marble bead, the twin of the one I'd left at the bothy below the standing stones on Barra. Was that really just yesterday? It seemed so long ago now. Placed carefully inside the top of the gatepost, the bead would be safe. The weathered wood gave the machair plain gravitas, a grainy voice amongst the Clovers and Daisies and Grasses, suggesting long-ago times when trees covered the Western Isles. As we left I noticed a bright yellow ear tag, number 00324, tucked into the wire that encircled the post, and I wondered if it belonged to our white-faced friend.

'Nice pair of horses,' the man said, laying down the wire strainers, stepping away from the fence.

'You'll need your hats on if you're headed that way.' The man was smiling, he had an open attractive face.

'The terns are nesting over by the next gateway. They're fearsome,' he said, laughing at our confused expressions. 'They've been frightening off walkers with their dive-bombing and their screeching. I'm Alasdair, by the way.'

He asked where we were headed for that night.

'We're staying in the hostel at Bowmore. Hopefully, there'll be room. You can't book ahead,' Shuna said, 'and someone called Chrissie in Drimisdale has a croft where we can put the ponies. We've been told to look out for a house with a red roof.'

'That will be my sister, Chrissie.'

'I haven't actually spoken to her, it was a woman called Beatrix who gave me her name,' Shuna said. 'Beatrix was going to have the ponies on her croft, but she was away until tonight and would have had to move her own horses. So she suggested Chrissie.'

'Aye, they'll be fine on Chrissie's croft. It stretches way out around the back. You've still quite a way to go though. How do you know Beatrix?'

'Well, I don't really.' Shuna laughed. 'She's the friend of a friend and gave us a contact for where the ponies stayed last night in Garrynamonie, and she sorted somewhere for us tonight. She's been really helpful.'

'They're good people, her boy helps me out a lot. He's mad for the crofting, great with machinery and a good help with everything. I work twenty-seven hours a week at the Military Range, the rest of the time, evenings, weekends, I'm doing this.' He spread his arms wide. 'I can always do with a good hand. The silage making, now that's a big job, there's a team of five of us, we do the contracting. I take a week off work in August, and a week off in September, and we pack in as many hours as the daylight and the weather will allow us.'

'And there's always fences to repair,' I said, nodding to the fence behind him.

'This is a township fence. We're getting 80 per cent grant to replace it, but see trying to get folks in a township to agree on anything.' He smiled. 'Impossible!'

'And then there's the sheep.' He pointed to the hills in the east.

'Beinn Hecla, Beinn Choradail, Beinn Mhor, they're twelve-hour days with the gathering and the clipping, and there's less and less that are able to do it. Nobody has dogs any more, and it's hard ground to gather.' He paused as we looked up into the hills, imagining.

'In the spring I spread seaweed with the muck-spreader. That's my machair share there.' He pointed to a patch that was

75

greening up nicely. I couldn't even begin to imagine how he got all this done.

'Where do you live then?' asked Shuna.

He nodded towards the ruins of Ormacleit Castle that were now to the south of us.

'I was born in that white house next to the castle. That's a Clan Ranald castle, the last castle built in Scotland, 1700. It was burned down, a roast of venison they say, just fifteen years after it was built. After the white house we moved into the house next to it, the one with no roof. After that I built my own.' He pointed to a bungalow a short distance from the other buildings.

'Do you ever get off the island? Do you have time?' I asked.

'Oh, you have to get off the island every now and then or you'd go mad. Casinos, that's where I go. On the mainland, sometimes America. I always say, if there was a casino on the island I'd have no shoes on my feet.' There was an easy smile on his face.

As he was talking, Mute Swans coasted on the loch behind him and a Sandpiper's three-note call wove through his softly-spoken sentences. I could have listened to him for hours but, like he said, we still had a way to go.

'Mind to put your hats on,' he called after us.

It must have been after 9pm by the time we reached Drimisdale. The evening was golden, windless, the sky almost cloudless. 'Lovely to be here without a midge in sight,' Shuna said. We both knew that at home a still evening like this would mean midges for sure. We watched an old man move his cows, patiently and slowly. The low-setting sun glinted off his two crutches. He looked like he'd been moving cows at the end of the day for a hundred years.

Chrissie's husband, Angus John, and his brother John met us in the Kawasaki Mule, an all-terrain buggy. Angus John had had a stroke ten years earlier which had left him partly paralysed.

The Mule was how he got about. 'Follow us,' he called cheerily as they sped away across the grass. We cantered to keep up, grinning across at each other. The ponies sensed the end of the day. Once we were on the road the brothers told us where to go and zoomed off ahead. A woman was walking briskly towards us. She was slim with silvered hair and, as she got closer, I saw she was wearing pink trainers and pink lipstick. Her eyes sparkled.

'Is one of you Shuna? I'm Beatrix. We're just back from the mainland. We were down at the Royal Welsh Show. Sorry you couldn't stay on the croft, but it was too complicated with the horses.' She walked beside us and chatted, stopping by a gate. 'Here I am, this is home, just keep going along there and you'll find Chrissie and Angus John.'

There was a strong family resemblance between Chrissie and her brother. She had the same warm open face. She showed us where to put the ponies and let us put our tack in her barn for the night, then offered us a lift round to the hostel.

As we bounced along in the Mule I told her about the man we'd seen with crutches, moving the cows.

'Ah, that's Father Time,' she said, 'that's what we call him. He'd have been putting the cows down to the machair for the night. That's the old way.'

We said our goodnights and headed towards the hostel, a renovated blackhouse with a thatched roof and whitewashed walls that glowed in the low light. Chrissie's words, *the old way*, were turning in my mind as Shuna pushed open the hostel door.

DAY SIX

Howmore to Iochdar

We walked slowly from the bunkhouse door, passing the row of stones that weighted down the tight roof thatch, towards the building where the kitchen was, and paused to take in the scene. It was a grey-silk morning with soft patches of mist lying over stone and bone. The crumpled curve of an old dyke, topped with a collection of weather-worn animal skulls, ran down towards gravestones which leaned softly towards the arched windows of the ancient chapels of Tobha Mòr.

The kitchen was a-clatter with busy breakfasters: the beautiful lookalike couple, both over six feet tall, slim, very blonde, wearing skin-clinging cycling gear who volleyed words of lightly veiled blame: 'It always rains when you plan our holiday'; the young German man travelling in a car; the middle-aged English man with an air of defiant aloneness. 'Using the buses,' he told us; the two cyclists from Stornoway, commercial divers, who talked about GoPros and beer and tight hamstrings. We ate our porridge outside and watched the beginnings of blue start to burrow into the grey sky. We'd added blueberries and chopped apple and honey to the porridge. Picking some fine white pony hairs from my porridge, I wondered what those early Christians had eaten for breakfast.

The sound of Snipe drumming over the lower marshy ground carried in the damp air. After coffee we wandered down towards the chapels. I let my fingers rest on bones – a cow's skull, a sheep's jaw – smooth and warmer than the air. The chapels were soft-edged with weather and lichen. In his book *Poacher's Pilgrimage* Alastair McIntosh describes these islands as being 'saturated in the twilight of sanctity'. This was a peaceful place, in the simple beauty of Dugald's Chapels I thought again of Mum's relationship with the Roman Catholic Church. Her grievances and sense of betrayal by those in the convents in Belgium and England who were supposedly caring for her, and by her own parents. When I asked my Uncle Kevin about his own and Mum's respective boarding school experiences, he'd said, 'They take away your childhood, and you spend the rest of your life trying to reclaim it.' A picture of Mum as a tiny girl floated into my mind: freckled, thin, long thick plaits, the softest smile breaking through. I remembered my grandmother, Mum's mother, looking at the picture with me and saying over my shoulder, 'I don't know what went wrong with your mother, she was the sweetest little girl...'

Shuna and I walked slowly back towards the hostel, just as 'using the buses' man arrived back. We'd seen him leave for the bus an hour earlier. 'No bus,' he said, shrugging. 'I'll try the next one.' He seemed happy enough to settle in the kitchen with a cup of tea and his book. It would be lovely to spend the day in this gentle place, I thought, but we needed to get going. We thanked Betty the warden when she turned up for her daily visit. She was full of the joys, and when she spotted our saddlebags we talked about ponies. She took us outside and pointed out her own Eriskay ponies, two precious brown dots on a faraway hillside.

We said our goodbyes, picked up our gear and set off towards Chrissie's croft. The saddlebags were heavy and we rested by a gate. I lay down on my back. I was taking better care of myself since having back surgery six years previously. There had been a time when I thought it was fine to push through pain, I did it for years in a job that I loved. As an equine podiatrist I spent a lot of time bent over under horses, trimming their feet. I'd felt at last that I'd found my career. Then, when Mum died, whatever had been holding my discs together gave way and splurged out. The next nine months were horrendous. As the pain became unbearable I took more and more painkillers, but as I took more pills my fear and sadness increased. Finally, I had surgery. It was my last resort, but I will never forget the immense gratitude I felt for that surgeon when I came round from the anaesthetic and the nerve pain had gone.

I was also very lucky with my friends and family, with Martin, keeping it all together. He must have been scared too, I don't remember him ever showing it, or complaining. And my friends, not least Shuna, who spent hours and hours on the phone, hearing my fears and my sadness. Really hearing me, and reassuring me. In her sitting room is a postcard titled, 'What is a friend? (…) He understands those contradictions in your nature that lead others to misjudge you (…) you can weep with him, sin with him, laugh with him, pray with him. Through it all – and underneath – he sees, knows and loves you. What is a friend? (…) Just one with whom you dare to be yourself.'

Cirrus-cloud rayed out above me and a strong breeze was blowing owl notes through the broken rungs of the gate. I stood up slowly and picked up the saddlebags. The ache in my lower back had eased. 'You good to go?' Shuna asked. I nodded.

Those ruptured discs in my back had changed my life. In her book *Braving the Wilderness* Brené Brown talks about the Buddhist term 'strong back, soft front'. She quotes Buddhist teacher and activist Joan Halifax: *All too often our so-called strength comes from fear, not love; instead of having a strong back, many of us have a defended front shielding a weak spine. In other words, we walk around brittle and defensive, trying to conceal our lack of confidence.* While Mum was dying, and then after her death, many of the stories I'd told myself about her, and myself, gradually dissolved.

I believe that my anger and mistrust towards her had been my armour, my 'defended front', and without it my back literally collapsed. I needed that physical and emotional breakdown to be able to build myself up again, from the spine out. It is also what led me to writing. My defences around Mum, and the intensely physical work of hoof-trimming, had been crutches. Without them I collapsed, and then, step by slow step a more creative path opened up to me.

We unbolted the heavy door into the barn where we'd left our tack the night before. The building had been built to last, had the best of fittings including a solid steel frame, and it felt like everything of importance on the croft was sheltering here from the weather.

'Look at this,' said Shuna, pointing at an L reg 'International' tractor, bonnet off and bleeding beads of oil onto the cardboard and spanners lying under its chassis. There were holes in the bodywork where rust had eaten all the way through. 'The tyres are brand new, never been used, look!' Shuna's fingers held out the threads of rubber still attached to the treads. The old tractor with its brand new tyres. Things were well cared for around here. I loved how Shuna's more practical eye picked out different things to mine.

There was a ride-on mower, a strimmer, galvanised cattle gates set up in the far corner, a sawhorse, piles of neatly stacked logs, bags of nitrate fertiliser, a sack barrow, plastic cockle baskets, dog beds and 45-gallon drums. Oiled top-links hung from a crossbeam and bottles of Round-Up sat high out of harm's way. There was a measuring wheel, windproof netting, a never-used garden rake, light boards for trailers with their cables wrapped round them, a set of drain rods and four smiling scarecrows, their lips stitched on in big looping smiles. The fur of a dead rat was a slash of poisoned weave against the concrete floor.

'Oh, wow, an Albion,' said Shuna. It looked antique, the name 'Albion' painted in elegant letters. A small cast-iron seat sat up high, reminding me of a distant memory; bare metal cold against my bum, feet dangling, small hands on a wobbly steering wheel.

'What is it?' I asked.

'A binder, I think, for oats, barley. Shian used to have one of these at the farm.' 'The farm' is on Loch Melford in Argyll, and is where Shuna has lived for the last twenty years building up a horse business. The farm is owned by Shian MacLean, in her eighties and still formidably active and impassioned about all things to do with the land. Months later Shuna sent me a link on Facebook to *Greylag: Corn: Crofter*, a creative documentary made by Beatrix whom we'd met the evening before. There was that same binder turning on a summer's evening, the air full of chaff caught in the dropping sun, and Alasdair and Chrissie and Beatrix's son working together with friendly focus.

We picked up our saddles and walked outside. The ponies were grazing nearby, their rumps towards us. A flock of chickens dotted around them, a mixture of Black Rocks and Red Rocks, their skirts lifting in the wind. 'Good morning, how are the ponies today?' Chrissie was wandering down from the house towards us. 'Will you come in for a cup of tea?' The three of us walked past a pile of freshly cut peats, an axe lying on top, past a quad bike and trailer and into their porch where a dozen duck eggs were incubating. A milky-eyed Collie followed us to the sitting room and flopped down with the suddenness that comes with worn-out joints. Angus John was in his wheelchair by the window, a cigarette sending delicate smoke signals across the view of Loch an Eileen to the hills beyond.

'Is that a dun on the island there?' I asked, sitting on the sofa beside John.

'No, that's a castle,' he said, reaching to put out his cigarette.

'Don't put it out on our account. I love the smell of tobacco,' I said. He looked surprised, brought it back to his mouth, and exhaling a cloud of smoke said, 'Aye, it's a castle, Caisteal Bheagram, and see that line of rocks there, on the other side, they're clapping stones. Do you know what they are?' He looked at me directly, his eyes bright. 'They're there to warn of anyone approaching. If you stand on them they tilt and make a clapping sound.'

'Clever,' said Shuna.

'What a great spot to build a house,' I said. 'You can see for miles'.

'It wasn't always like this. Fifteen of us brought up in a thatched cottage. It wasn't easy. And you know something, all of us are still living.'

'Fifteen of you!' I said.

'Oh, there was some that had more than fifteen children. Do you remember, John, the McGoughans, they had twenty.'

Their surname was Laing. 'From De Laing, the first Jacobite fighters who came over from France,' John told us. The two brothers talked about the Jacobite Uprising and the Highland Clearances as if they'd been there themselves. They spoke of 'Butcher Cumberland' with as much detail as they described their schoolteacher who used to come to school in a kilt, who'd worn a full beard to hide his bullet wounds from the First World War. Their sentences slid up and down the centuries like fingers on the chanter.

'Have a good trip down North,' Chrissie said as we pulled our boots back on. 'Down North', how curious, I thought, as we walked towards the ponies.

While we'd been inside the wind had strengthened and now, early afternoon, following fences towards the shore, my map case was being spun on its cord until it jammed tight. Manes whipped the backs of our hands. We didn't even try to talk as rain hit our faces. It was wind with a capital W like in Chrys Salt's poem *The Island*: 'It is all Wind, all of it –/ripping thatch/ from roofs; earth from grass roots;/ scattering stacks/plucking fence-wire to a jangled/bent disharmony./Slicing the sky to tattered rag above/Corghadal, Hecla and Ben More.'

The beach that took us almost all the way to Iochdar was marked 'danger area' in red on the OS map. The Laings had said we'd be fine as long as the flags were down. If they were up it meant they might be firing missiles from the range. There was no sign of the flags, but nonetheless we kept a keen eye out as we rode along. The wind was behind us, flinging sand between the ponies' legs and against our waterproofs. It was a low-slung sky and we kept our eyes looking downwards, our hands in our pockets, buffs pulled up over our mouths, hoods pulled up over our riding hats. My stomach had been rumbling for a while. I thought about the drovers of old who'd walked cattle from all corners of Uist onto boats to the mainland, then over the hills to Crieff or further South. They and their dogs would head off with little more than some oatmeal to eat. Hardy beyond belief.

When it started to rain heavily again, we left the beach looking for somewhere sheltered to eat lunch. An empty silage pit hidden in the dunes, and its high walls offered some protection from the wind and rain careering up from the south. We ate yesterday's spaghetti reborn with a can of sardines and a few drops of Tabasco. After lunch we stuck to the dunes as they offered some shelter. Rabbits sprang up underfoot and, on the skyline, appeared what looked like giant lamp posts. As we rode closer we saw they were floodlights and there were sky-grey bunkers. It was an airstrip. A jeep zoomed towards us and as it got closer it veered off the runway and bounced over the dunes, barely slowing, to come to a sudden stop nearby, against the high fence.

'Oh, shit,' said Shuna.

A man in overalls got out. Alasdair on his day job. He told us they'd been watching us from the tower for ages, 'and no, it was fine, no testing today'. After he sped off we meandered on through the dunes, passing mats of old silage in hollows where they fed cattle in the winter. Feeding spots out of the wind with sandy soil to keep hooves and legs dry. I thought of how we struggled at home to keep the cattle out of mud which seemed to get worse each year. I had serious sandy-soil envy.

'What's that noise?' Shuna asked. I pushed my hood back. It sounded like something vast and mechanised was about to come crashing over the dunes at us. I was actually ducking down, my heart in my mouth, as we trotted up the bank in time to see a raft of camouflage quad bikes racing past us on the beach. They were very close but none of the soldiers saw us, intent as they were on racing down the beach, and maybe having a tough time seeing through the wind and rain. We walked the ponies onto the sand feeling relieved. 'That was surreal,' I said. Ringed Plovers scattered at the wave-edges like our adrenalin-fired thoughts. I got off Ross to walk for a while and warm up my joints.

We followed the tread-marks and sand-spittings from the quad bikes. White horses surged into shore under a flat mono-chrome sky. Oystercatchers anchored themselves on widely spaced legs. All across the beach were little monuments: shells and pebbles, upstanding, the sand swept from around their bases by the wind. I picked up Limpet shells (only the ones with holes in their tops) and stacked them in my palm as I walked. There were other things on this beach: a blue rubber glove, a piece of plastic tape that said *Arctic Fish Processing*, a shock of fluorescent orange netting. Before leaving the beach I threaded the Limpet shells, Mum's beads for the day, one by one over stems of Marram Grass, little collaborations of tenacity for her, before walking slow-footed onto the road to Iochdar and the home of Billy McPhee, 'the gentle accordionist'.

'What's the plan?' asked the cheery man who met us on the road. Billy asked that question numerous times during our stay with him. We quickly learnt he wasn't looking for an answer. From the get-go he had lots of plans, and Shuna and I were very happy to 'go with the flow', which was something else he liked to say. 'I'm teaching an accordion lesson at 6.30, they'll be here any minute. Can you cook?' Another rhetorical question. He thrust a wok into my arms and began to fill it with food: two packets of chicken breasts, three onions from the cupboard, a packet of Uncle Ben's 'perfect in 2 minutes' rice, a jar of Sharwood's Balti Cooking Sauce and tubs of nutmeg, garam masala and cinnamon. There was also a packet of smoked salmon and two cans of Baxter's Cream of Tomato and Lobster Bisque.

'Cooking is no problem,' we said. 'Dinner at seven then?'

We left his house clutching our hoard and crossed the yard, past his grandparents' milking shed that he was converting into his 'music hub', in through the kitchen door of a warm bungalow. 'It belongs to my brother,' Billy had said when we arrived. 'You'll be better in here than in my house. I'll just turn the camera off.' We'd watched him cross to the windowsill in the living room and fiddle with a gadget positioned on the windowsill.

'Camera?' I asked

'Aye, means my brother can look at the view when he's in Glasgow, almost like he's here, you know.' Shuna and I were touched beyond words.

We set about cooking tea. We dug about in our saddlebags

and added a lemon, the ubiquitous Tabasco and some pepper to the mix of ingredients. We reflected on our blowy day and passed the hip flask between us as we cooked.

'So, what's the plan? Let's go for a drive, I want to show you a few things.' Billy had finished his dinner and was already standing up, laughing. He was a whirlwind of enthusiasm. He and Shuna hadn't stopped talking about traditional music and people they both knew in that world. It turned out also that Billy, like Shuna, was a fan of Angus McPhee, but had never heard about the stone on the beach here in Iochdar that Shuna had read about. The one Angus had carved his initials on before he went off to war. 'I think you'll need to stay another night so we can find out about the stone. I'll ask about. You'll need to go to the museum too. Where are you going next?'

'Grimsay.'

'No need to be in a hurry to get to Grimsay. There's a lot to see here. Let's do a tour before it's dark. The weather's not up to much, but you'll get a feel for the place.'

The three of us got into the front of his little white van and Tess, his Border Collie, jumped in the back. Ross and Chief were eating in a very green field, where neither sheep nor cattle competed for the grass. We passed shrines to the Virgin Mary already lit up in the darkening light.

'Iochdar is made up of lots of parts,' said Billy. 'Each one has a different name, and each one has a shrine.' We turned right at the main road and headed south. Water glimpsed grey on each side of the main road, we were in the middle of fresh water now, it was all so different from the coastline we'd ridden north along. Hundreds of Mute Swans lightened the surface of Loch Bì.

'Our Lady of the Isles,' Billy said, taking a sharp left and driving steeply up towards a mast. 'You need to have a wee look.' We looked down on the giant statue, glowing white in the half-light. 'That's a Hugh Lorimer statue,' he said. 'Put up to protect the island when the Rocket Range was coming in the fifties. The money that was left over paid for all the wee shrines you've seen. It was at the time of the Cold War, you see. People were worried.'

Once back on the main road we took another road to the left signed for Loch Sgioport. 'It's a very special place down here,' said Billy. 'See what you think, but for me, well, I think it's very special.' He opened the driver's side window and cool peaty air rushed in. 'This is Loch Druidibheag. I do a lot of fishing here, the trout have Ferox genes, you know, cannibal. I come out with a rod, it's very productive.' The loch was a mass of tiny islands, an in-between world of peat and water and wide-flung stepping stones.

'What's that?' I asked, spotting stone walls on a promontary.

'That's a sheep fank. Yes, sheep out here, but not so many now. There's the "Sheep Club", they joke it should be called "The Not Quite Gone Club" now.' He chuckled. 'All this belongs to Grogarry Lodge, it's a hunting and fishing estate. See there, the white branches, that's where they're poisoning the rhododendrons. Crazy, isn't it, those rich Victorians planted them, now we're paying to take them out. They inject them, you know. And see there, kaboom, a monkey puzzle tree, out here!'

The road weaved between rising hills. 'Look!' said Shuna, pointing to two small bay ponies up ahead.

'Aye, there's a herd of about forty-five,' said Billy. 'Shetlands they are, just run wild, friendly as anything. They'll come to the window in a second. Wait 'til you see this.' He stopped alongside them. They were right there with their muzzles, breath steaming in the cold damp air. Their manes and forelocks were magnificent, thick and dreadlocked, streaked with highlights the colour of last year's deer grass.

'Oh, they're gorgeous,' said Shuna.

We carried on to the end of the tarmac road. Billy pointed at the track that continued between side cuttings. 'The sea's just over there, the old pier, very steep down the other side.' Months later I read in Terry J. Williams' book *Walking with Cattle* how the cattle used to be driven from the machair on the west, never having seen a bog before and wanting to run for home, down over this steep hill onto the waiting boat. Reading about the skill of the drovers and their dogs was humbling. Reading about the horrors the cattle must have gone through was harrowing.

'Come and have a look at this.' Billy got out of the van. 'See that house across there, that's a ruin now, but the Aga's still there, everything in it just as it was. Folks lived there until the fifties. It was hard, they used to walk out to church once a week and get a lift back. I know one of the brothers who was brought up there. He won't talk about those years.'

On the way back, as the hills gradually lost themselves against the night sky, Billy talked about the Clearances. How it wasn't just for sheep and changing land use that people were moved off. It was religious too. He talked about families being moved from here to there on account of what religion they were, and then others being moved in to the vacuum. Folks being put on harder and harder ground on the east, how they 'had to take to the fishing, those who had never fished, and aye, there were the sheep too.' He listed place names and family names, and again I was struck with the immediacy of the past and the closeness of family. 'That's where my grandfather on my father's side is from.' I got lost in place names and family names and the passing blur of rhododendron skeletons as we drove on, before reaching the main road and heading south again. I listened sleepily as Billy and Shuna chatted: 'Old Fred McCauley, now he brought Gaelic Radio from long wave to FM.' 'The Marquis of Bute, he did good work, he built the hospital, this hospital, The Sacred Heart Hospital.'

My heart thumped as two Owls flew low over the ground on my side of the van. 'What owls are they?'

'Short Eared Owls. South Uist is famous for them,' Billy said. The soft sight of them took my thoughts to Anglesey, to my grandparents' house and the stuffed Barn Owl in the hall. To Anglesey, never my favourite place but Nain and Taid had been there, and I'd adored them. To me they'd been warm and stable and loving. They'd had us children every Wednesday when Mum was at college in Bangor. They gave us fish fingers and Grenadine in milk. We'd had strict bedtimes and our own patch of flower bed each to plant. I'd felt safe there. Life with Mum was chaotic. She had a wild heart and was always up to all sorts. Shortly after my fourth birthday, early days in Anglesey, 'the Irish' moved in. Two young hitchhikers she had picked up. They stayed with us for a while, laughed a lot, drank a lot. They had both been Mum's lovers, I learned many years later. They poured a bucket of cold water over me in the bath one night. Laughed and laughed. I shuddered at the memory.

'I know it's getting dark, but I want to show you one more place: Lochboisdale. I'll say no more, see what you think.' Billy wanted to show us the results of a £12 million development. 'Good for Marine Harvest, the yachting world, no one else though. We're all waiting for stage two, if it ever comes.' The place felt lifeless, the lettering FAILTE dripped over boarded-up shop windows. The Tourist Information Centre was closed, the bank too. The hotel was hanging on.

'The job's only half done,' he continued, 'then various councils ship in folks from housing in Dunoon and Lochgilphead, people mostly with problems, you know. The poor souls, stuck out here with nothing, not even a shop, and most can't drive, and the bus service is shite.' He paused. 'That's enough. I just wanted you to see it. Now, let's go back and have a beer.'

Before the turning to Iochdar we veered sharply to the right.

'Just one more place, one more place.' Billy pointed to a track disappearing across a peat moor. 'That's where Angus McPhee went to get his peats. There's a story, that one day his father wouldn't let him take the horse, so do you know what he did? He pulled the cart himself, that's what he did. They say he was a strong, strong man.'

It was fully dark by the time we got back to Iochdar. Billy looked at the clock and turned on the radio, leaning in close. 'I want to catch the news. The girls in Manchester,' he said, 'the two girls from Barra, there's still no news...' The shrines blinked at us as we approached his house and he told us about the bombing at the Ariana Grande concert the day before. 'Terrorism, they're saying. ISIS.' He said that two girls from Barra were missing, that he was glad he lived where he lived now, that the world was so troubled. In that moment, on the western shore of South Uist, the world suddenly felt very small.

DAY SEVEN
Staying in Iochdar

Back in the bungalow, bacon and a snuggle of mushrooms sizzled on the gas cooker. Billy had driven us down to Garrynamonie before starting work and we'd come back in Shuna's pickup. I was buzzing after seeing another Short Eared Owl. Sitting on a fencepost by the roadside, her wings lifting out behind her, eyes huge – so close, daffodil yellow – searing into me. We'd decided to take Billy's advice, 'to go with the flow and look around', and were staying in Iochdar for another night. The ponies would get a day off. We planned to visit the Museum at Kildonan, and there was also a woodland at Loch Eynort that Morag had told us about. 'The life's work of a single man, an amazing place you need to see,' she'd said. 'A modern-day Callum's Road.'

I cracked two eggs into the frying pan and watched the ponies grooming each other, soft shapes in the morning mist. Above them the shed's corrugated roof bit into the air with scallop-edged rust. I opened the window and the rasping call of Corncrakes drifted in. Patches of Flag Irises gave them cover. The calls were the males attracting a female. Apparently after only two weeks the female abandons her crakelings to fend for themselves, finds a new partner and raises yet another brood.

That rasping reminded me of Tiree, the island where Martin

and I and the children had spent many family holidays, and I felt wistful. Three weeks was a long time to be away. I'd never had a problem before with being away from home. It always did me good. I was surprised by the intensity of that ache, but the corncrakes were chafing at my heart. Mum had travelled a lot when we were little, business trips selling seafood, and the jewellery trips. Selling her work and buying beads. I think I'd always experienced anxiety when she was away: a deep-down fear that she wouldn't come back. I hoped it had never been like that for my own children. Turning the eggs in the pan I soothed myself remembering words a Spanish friend had once said to me. 'You know Leonie, you are *una aguila*, and eagles need to fly from their nest, but they always come back.'

However we interpret it, there is nothing surer than history has as much to do with the present as the past, said the display board on the wall at Kildonan Museum. I pressed my hand into the unyielding body of a seaweed mattress and sat on the bench beside it, a 'being' in Gaelic. *On the being you will find carved the initials JM, where Iain Aonghais Ruaidh (John Morrison) tested out his sheep brand, having just pulled the glowing tongs from the fire. That mark could very well symbolise what this whole place is about: people's lives etched out of the past for the sake of the future.* I sat there for a few minutes, taking it all in.

Shuna was reading a sign that was leaning against the wall: *Angus created hats, jackets, boots, scarves, slippers, ropes, bridles and horse nose-bags from grass, leaves and sheep's wool. He wore grass hats and placed his creations around the trees and bushes in the hospital grounds.*

'I asked at the desk, nobody here knows about Angus McPhee's initials either but, guess what, they're re-doing the exhibition of his work. It's all in the storeroom at the moment.

The man at the desk said if we come back just before 5.00 he'll let us see it!' I smiled as much at her delight as at the invite. Later, true to his word, the objects were laid out on a table where we would touch them, and smell them. Still hay-sweet after all these years. We would feel lucky beyond words to look at the mass of woven grasses, worn soft and loose over the decades like slept-on plaits, and admired a traditional Uist horse collar, and a broom, its kinked heather twigs bound with woollen twine.

'How about we go and see the rest of the exhibition?' I asked. 'Then head out to Loch Eynort?' We walked through a room with Victorian artefacts: a telescopic silver toasting fork *found in Boisdale House, used by Lady Gordon Cathcart's family*; a walking stick *probably 19th century, made from snake's vertebrae*; two deer's feet turned into ornaments. I shuddered, but Mum would have loved these things. Her eyes would have gleamed the way they did when she found something fascinating, the more peculiar the better. She loved Victorian workmanship, had a collection of oddities like snakeskin purses. She had a thing about animal skins and fur and wore her mother's mink coat defiantly with a flash of 'don't you dare judge me' in her expression. She loved ivory too, and would buy old ivory billiard balls and make beads out of them. She said it might as well be used, but of course she'd never touch modern ivory. She'd made ivory buttons for Stevie Wonder in the shape of Africa back in the eighties. I remember her telling me that as a child she used to skin animals, moles and voles. She'd tan the hides, save them and make them into things. She was very pragmatic and very creative.

Shuna and I walked through the exhibition, past spinning wheels and weaving looms and skeins of wool. We stopped in front of a display on natural dyes. I recognised some of the beautiful Lichens we'd been riding past; the gold one splashed over the rocks, *Old Man's Beard – Feasag Nan Creag*, and next to it a picture of *Black Crotal – Crotal Dubh* – used for the original Harris Tweed brown colour. The recipe was *4 ounces black crotal, 4 pints peaty water*. I read how the Crotal Dubh was *scraped off the rocks with a metal spoon, the dye was made in a large iron communal dyeing pot by adding layers of fleece and Crotal and left to simmer for hours*. There was a photograph of *Yellow Crotal – Crotal Bhuidhe* which changes to indigo in sunlight *Gold on the rock/Purple in the pot*. There were loops of wool pinned up, all different colours – beside the picture of Iris roots the wool was a gentle orange. There were also dye recipes for Bog Myrtle and Nettle, even soot: *A half pound of soot produced by peat and coal/4 pints water/Iron mordant from rusty metal/Simmer for a half hour*. This concoction dyed the wool a goldeny olive colour. I left that place feeling not only steeped in the past but also the secrets of plants.

The sign read 'Arinaban Woodland'. There was an arrow pointing to the north and a thick black outline of the croft filled in with green for the woodland area. Bubble letters spelt out 'CROFT No 8, 5 KMS PATHWAYS THRO' CROFT. S's written on the map showed seats, T's indicated tables. We walked along footpaths that curved Bluebell-scented through Birches and Rowans, and passed ruins now sheltering a nursery for the trees, a square of earth sown with tatties. Thickets of wild Brambles shimmered with birdsong. One path led to a bay where a boat called 'Silkie' was moored in a stone-built nook between woodland and loch. The tide was out and she was tilting on the shore. I peeped into the cabin to see newspapers spread on the table, curled yellow with damp and age. I couldn't see the date but had a feeling it had been a long time since the boat had been out in the loch. Beyond 'Silkie' we levered an ingenious lead-weighted pulley system to get over a stile and onto a bridge. The air was dense with the scent of Hawthorn blossom, sweet and musky as ferrets. Bees sucked nectar from mauve-speckled stamens. We walked towards an inlet where two Ducks guddled along a channel of water that curled silver through the tidal mud. Further out a Heron flew due east drawing wing-slow time in the water beneath.

On the way back, following a higher path, we came to a rock like a curved oyster shell. We sat in silence feeling grateful to the man who had placed this rock here. To the man who had made all these paths, grown the trees from seed and planted them. Who had dug earth and woven driftwood fences. A rhythmical clanging broke through the birdsong and a tall man appeared, one metal spike balanced on his right shoulder, another being used as a walking stick. Each step was marked by a metallic clank.

'Lovely stone,' I said, patting the seat as the man approached.

He paused, planting the walking spike.

'Aye, my father had to sit on that one over there.' He nodded behind us. 'He liked to rest up here, but that stone wasn't very comfortable so I brought this one down.'

'How did you move it?'

'With my wee digger.'

We watched him walk off. He was so broad that the spike rested on a plateau of shoulder. He was all bone, no flesh to spare, no coat either.

Before the path dropped to the car park we came to more rocks, great hewn slabs of granite arranged on top of each other. I struggled to imagine how a 'wee digger' would lift them. Like Stone Age Man this man had secrets too. The stone facing me had *AD* carved into it in letters a foot high. I touched the rock nearest me, a granite block with seams of quartz tipping over the edge. Around the other side two M's were carved into it. It rested on two perpendicular slabs with grooves channelling

99

down at a 45° angle. Shuna and I discussed whether these rocks might have been part of a pier at one time, and these indentations were for the ropes to run along. I pulled the bead purse from my pocket and chose a small quartz lozenge with a spiral twist carved around it. I rested it at the lip of one of the grooves, knowing that when I let go it would roll into the darkness between the two carved M's. *U for underneath, spells MUM,* I thought to myself.

Down near the car park were a group of men with fat-legged tripods. I asked the nearest one what they were doing.

'Birdwatching,' he said, with a German accent.

'Seen anything exciting?'

'No, a disappointing day,' he said, his words heavy. We carried on and met another man walking towards us. He had a beaming smile and was balancing a tripod on his shoulder. Another shoulder, another passion. He told us he was running a birdwatching tour, that the group were his clients. I asked him what the small ducks I'd seen on Druidibheag Loch last night might have been.

'Probably Tufted Duck.' I was happy to have a name. He was happy to share.

We drove away past a single Clydesdale-type horse, big-boned and rangy as the tree-planting man back there. We passed boulder fields and Red Stags, deep granite-time meshing with antlers-in-velvet time. I passed Shuna an apple and bit into my own.

Billy McPhee was on the phone when we drove into his yard. He moved towards us, his voice carrying clearly.

'So, I've talked to Angus McPhee's nephew, Ian Campbell. He knows where the initials are on the shore. So, that's Shuna and Beady just got back now. I'll take them down, we'll head off there now. Okay, *ma ha.* Talk later.'

He looked delighted as he put his phone back in his pocket. 'Right then, did you get the gist of that? So that's the plan, let's go, let's go.'

John Campbell pulled on a padded checked shirt as he stepped out of the house. He was a big man with a kind strong-browed face. He stepped familiarly into guide mode. This clearly wasn't the first time he'd been asked to show people the rocks.

'The shore was our playground when we were children,' he explained, opening a gate next to a farm shed. 'That house,' he pointed to a dilapidated thatched cottage on our left, 'that's where Angus McPhee was brought up.' He tapped the wall on his right. 'But he was born here, in the long house that was knocked down to build this shed. Right here he was born.'

We walked towards the thatched cottage. Two chimneys were still upright, bare roof rafters bridged brokenly between them with clods of peat-brown thatch slumping across. A heavy rope fell from beside each of the two windows and ran along the ground beneath the doorway, like a sad but not unwelcoming smile. I walked around to the gable end where the rope hung at thatch height and got out my bead purse for the second time that day. I chose a ceramic bead, robin's egg blue, with an iridescent sheen. As I threaded the bead onto its silk and wove it through the rope, I could hear the others chatting.

'He'd weave when we brought him back for the weekends from Uist House,' Ian said. 'I'd collect him grass.'

'Marram?' asked Shuna.

'No, any grass, like from the side of the road. He did talk, you know. They say he didn't, but he'd always talk to people who were over his shoulder. People we couldn't see. He'd have a right good laugh with them.'

I thought of Chrys Salt's poem *The Burning* about Angus McPhee: '*I am not mad*'/he says/inside his head/'*Madness is only longing*'/turned inward like a thorn.

I finished tying off the bead remembering Paul's voice shouting at Mum, *You're fucking mad.* Him telling her she had to see a psychotherapist or he'd leave her. She went in the end, got appointments on the NHS, and for a long time visited her 'trick cyclist' weekly at The Crichton in Dumfries. I never thought Mum was mad, but a thorn of longing turned inward makes sense to me. Her longing to be loved, to be celebrated, to be seen, to be creative, above all to be free. I wondered if she was soothed by those hundreds, no thousands, of hours threading beads, knotting silk thread between pearls, taking time and care to create beautiful things. Her fingers and her imagination showing the delicacy and the burn of her heart, thorn or no thorn.

Ian's face broke into a wide smile as he bent down to walk through the low doorway.

'I was brought up in this house, my three brothers and my sister in this room, and my parents in the closet, here in the kitchen. We had a flat black stove, what a difference that made, and the electric of course. When we got that it changed everything. I remember feeding coins into the meter up there.' He pointed to a fuse and meter still on the wall. Beside me, fat electrical cables ran up from a light switch, the old kind, like a breast, I thought, its nipple angled downwards to the broken floor.

'Angus McPhee's grandfather built this to last. The beams were bought in, but the rest of the wood was collected from the shore.'

We followed him out of the cottage and down to the sea. The tide was out, perfect timing. 'It's somewhere hereabouts,' he said, walking carefully across the slippery slabs of rock.

'Ah, here.' He cupped seawater in his palms from a rock pool and splashed it over the black stone. Immediately letters glistened in sharp relief, *AMP*, strong evenly spaced initials carved by the steady hand of a man as yet unbroken by war. A square was engraved around it, a framed glimpse into a moment seventy-seven years before. On a slab nearby the initials of another Iochdar man, Angus Bowie, carved in 1914, who hadn't come home from the First World War. His initials had been there for over a hundred years. All those tides, in and out. Tears slipped down my cheeks.

'Here are my own initials,' Ian said, walking on, 'and my daughters'.' Theirs are all here somewhere too.' He chuckled. I stepped slowly over the rocks amongst the initials carved by generations. Tiny sproutings of Bladderwrack, mustard gold against the black rock, glistened where they found footholds in the engravings. All around, Limpets were holding fast. On an impulse I pushed one with my thumb, as hard as I could. It didn't budge.

DAY EIGHT

Iochdar to Balivanich, Benbecula

Two Redshanks bobbed their heads on the dyke and spun the space between them with alerting calls. Today was a different kind of day, the mist had lifted and suddenly we saw what had been hidden behind a bank of cloud for the past two days. Standing in Billy's field, halters in hand, three duns rose out of the marshland. They seemed to quiver in the early sunshine and drew our eyes towards a stone circle beyond. The Redshanks' calls balanced centuries, millennia, on each press of notes. In Gaelic folklore the Redshank, a wading bird equally happy in water and on land, is seen as being able to travel between worlds. This world and the afterlife.

Leaning my back against the dyke I looked over towards the stone circle and wondered if Mum had come to this place during one of her visits. Whether, if she were alive now, we'd be able to go for a coffee, visit stone circles, hang out. Whether I would be able to smile, not wince, every time she called me 'darling', not flinch when she touched me. Whether I'd be able to simply love her and spend time with her. But I think I knew I was spinning a fantasy. Yes, I would be able to simply love her now, but that was because I was different, and one of the main reasons for that was her death. It had changed me in so many ways. If she was still alive, I just wouldn't be this exact same person wrapped in the Redshanks' song and feeling the sun glance over my hot tears. Why had it been so painful for us? Why had our relationship been a whetstone for us to sharpen claws and swords on?

I felt something smooth under my right hand. An upturned wine glass was slotted between the stones. Would whoever put it there come back one sun-spilt evening, turn it the right way up and fill it with chilled white wine. If I was staying another night, I might have done that. My Uncle Kevin once said to me, 'I loved Kathryn, Kathryn loved me. She was my sister. But she was a dreadful mother.' I could toast to my dreadful mother, and to my dreadful daughterly self, to the two of us behaving dreadfully, and to the two of us doing our absolute dreadful best.

Seven months after being on South Uist, and almost seven years to the day after Mum died, I saw Gyoto Tibetan monks performing with piper Griogair Laurie in Ballachulish Hall. Griogair opened the evening with a pipe lament which he'd learned from a sound recording of Callum Johnson, a *bodach* from Barra. It was about the Redshank, Griogair explained to us, and the only title he had for it was 'pee lil lee io', which is onomatopoeic of its song.

The pipes always make me think of Mum. She loved them, and that night in Ballachulish the hairs had stood up on the back of my neck as Griogair invoked the song of the Redshank. He brought to life with his music that liminal space between worlds, and set us up perfectly for the chanting of the Gyoto Tibetan monks. That evening I heard, for the first time, what musicologists call 'angel music', the note an octave and a third higher than their chanting that is created by harmonising. The Tibetans say that this 'angel music' is a frequency range which enables their deities and ancestors to be present, and the transmission of their teachings. They say it can help us connect with the true thread of our existence, to what gives our lives its meaning and where we can experience our full potential.

Driving home that night from Balachulish I felt every cell in my body full of love and life and music. I felt a strong sense of still being on a journey with Mum, that our relationship was alive and ongoing, and remembered a vivid moment in my childhood. We were living in Anglesey so I must have been six or seven years old and excited to be one of the angels in the school nativity play. Mum sat at the sewing machine, her red hair hanging over her wrists as she repositioned material under the needle. She was making ivory satin wings for me, but it turned out we were all to be the same, us angels, that we were to wear off-white nylon shifts. What most stuck in my memory, and made me saddest of all on the way back from Ballachulish that night, was remembering the relief I'd felt. Relief that I would be like the other children, that I wouldn't stand out. I can remember Mum's disdain of the teachers, *no bloody imagination*. She had always been amazing like that, wanting me to shine. It wasn't her fault that I'd wanted to hide. *The world is your oyster*, she'd say to me when I was older, or, another favourite of hers, *life isn't a dress rehearsal*. I'd respond with tight-mouthed sceptisim, but she'd been right. Life isn't a dress rehearsal. Bring on those wings.

Everything was shimmering as we set off that May morning from Billy's croft. The Irises were a dense yellow and the roofs of the barns slanted their deep ox-blood hue. Soon we would be crossing the tidal flats between South Uist and Benbecula. The sun was shining and the tide was going out. 'Cast with care' said a sign, warning fishermen about the overhead electricity wires.

'The girls from Barra,' Billy said, his face full of sorrow. 'They've confirmed that one is dead, and the other one is in hospital in a critical condition.' We'd stopped at his workplace, Hebridean Jewellery, for a goodbye coffee. The ponies were tied up outside. The cafe was filled with sunlight. John, the previous owner of Hebridean Jewellery, came in to fill his Tupperware. 'Best coffee on the island,' he told us proudly. His eyes were the same green as the aventurine earrings I'd seen in the shop. I'd been thinking about buying them but after the Barra news it didn't feel right. I left with the memory of John's eyes instead.

Outside, while we untied the ponies, Billy pointed out our route to us.

'You need to listen carefully. I've been asking about, and this is the route you need to take over the sand.' We took detailed note of the landmarks, the lines we needed to take across the sand, the tidal channels to avoid.

'It's much more complicated than it used to be, the causeway has affected the tidal patterns.'

The well-rested ponies had an enthusiastic swing in their steps as we rode across the expanse of wet sand sown with Worm casts. We were heading north using the tiny green-topped island of Heisteamuil, and the township of Lionacleit, as landmarks. A single wind turbine flashed brightly on the Benbecula shore. In the distance Eabhal bit a shapely chunk out of the sky over North Uist. The ponies' hooves started sinking as we rode along the edge of a deep scoop of tidal channel where the sand was laid down in tiny hillocks and marbled in black. It was as if volcanic ash had scattered over this world of sand hills. I got off Ross, struck by the patterns in the sand and wanting to look more closely. My feet sank unnervingly but stopped after an inch or two. Ross shifted his weight on the glutinous surface. I took the bead purse out of my pocket and chose a flat ceramic bead, about the size of a ten-pence piece. It was turquoise with five splashes of that flag-iris yellow. I chose another bead, the same yellow, but with a petroleum-swirl running through it, and laid them both down on the inky sand, knowing that very soon they would be lifted by the sea. I wondered where the currents would take them, how far these bright beads would shift with each tide. Imagining them separating, making their own way, their different shapes and weights influencing their separate paths. I got back on Ross and rode away, listening to each squelch and drag of the hooves. I turned in the saddle, our footprints had already smoothed themselves out, not a trace of the four of us left.

The sand got wetter and the ponies were sinking in more at each step. Ross stopped and swept the ground ahead with his muzzle, inhaling deeply. He was right, we'd drifted off course. We took our bearings and got back onto the route Billy had pointed out, crossing a deep tidal channel before stepping with relieved smiles onto dry sand on the other side. We looked back to where we had come from, shielding our eyes against the sun. The far shore looked a long way away. A little further round the coast we set up the stove, put the kettle on and celebrated crossing the South Ford with a cup of Earl Grey. The four of us were still, happy to soak up sunshine and the liquid song of Skylarks.

Continuing north with a warm southerly wind on our backs, we sometimes had to ride through croft land where we were careful to stick to the edges of the fields. Twite trilled beyond sturdy fences and well-hung gates. We'd entered a whole new land: no binder twine or wooden palettes or bed-ends here. Galvanised steel gates were all hung to within a millimetre of perfection. Disconcerted by this sudden change, I found myself missing the makeshift spirit of South Uist and Barra. Even the

Marram Grass seemed more efficient here, its roots binding the sand more firmly, the inward-furl of its leaves tighter. The beaches were empty and swept smooth by the wind, pristine surfaces marked only by the occasional well-rounded pebble. Needing to leave a bead on that scene of perfection, I chose a green jade one, small and round and polished. Placing it in the smooth concavity of one of Ross's hoof prints, I knew again that both would soon be taken by the tide, that disarray was never too far away.

It must have been five o'clock when we rode into Balivanich. Its Gaelic name Baile A'Mhanaich means 'town of the monks' after the monastery built there in the sixth century. It was a busy town, the main centre for North and South Uist, with an airport, hospital and a military base. As we rode past the airport I recognised the people in a car coming towards us, Fergus and his mum Dorothy. Fergus was at school with my daughter in Plockton, studying traditional music. I waved. There was a moment of recognition as they drove past, looking as if they were in a hurry. They lived on Grimsay and we would be heading their way the next day so hopefully we'd catch up then. The passing car was a reminder that we'd taken time out of our lives to do this journey, and that we were travelling at a very different pace. I felt a pang of guilt at the indulgence of it, felt a familiar wash of shame. *This is your thing, Beady, don't feel bad, just don't go there*. I knew how precious it was, this time travelling with ponies. That it was an opportunity to feel fully alive, to catch the thread of my life and let it run lightly through my fingertips, to feel its pull. So, smile at the car going by. *Let it go, Beady*.

We passed a group of men in army uniform who waved at us cheerily, the smell of frying chips teased from an open window and soon we saw the signs for 'Uist Community Riding School'. Happy, healthy horses grazed in paddocks and raised their heads in greeting. We were both looking forward to meeting the manager, Sue. She pulled into the yard shortly after we arrived, jumped out of her 4x4 and came towards us with a full uncomplicated smile. She showed us around and then shot off to 'cut some grass', just one of her many jobs. How she managed to run a riding centre as well as everything else she did was a mystery. She put it down to having a fantastic team of volunteers and enthusiastic children. Later on, over a cup of tea, she told us that she'd first come to Uist when working as a lorry driver and had fallen in love with the place. As a child her family would box the ponies from their home in Devon up to Glen Feshie in Perthshire every summer. Her father had loved Scotland and had passed that passion on to Sue.

'I was never going to settle anywhere else,' she said.

We slept that night on the floor of her office. It was a strange place after Sue left. She seemed to take the warmth with her, and an insidious damp slunk in once her back was turned. The centre at one time had been an army swimming pool and diving training facility. I lay fitfully with my back to the door that opened onto a cold dark passageway, where a creeping chill would spread across my back and wake me every time I fell asleep. Shuna had wisely bagged the space furthest from the door.

Perhaps it was the redshank song of that morning opening up other worlds to me. Long-forgotten memories pushed their way in as I held my eyes wide open in the darkness. Mum telling me that I used to see ghosts on the walls of my bedroom in the house at St Cyrus where we'd lived when I was a baby. She said she'd come into the room and find me screaming at the wall. Mum had seen the ghosts sometimes too. They were 'horrible creatures', she'd said, 'running over the wall'. She also told me she'd taken acid in that house when she'd had friends visit, and that while she was tripping she saw me being put into the oven.

She never took acid again. I tried turning my thoughts to other things, to the baby Oystercatchers Shuna and I had seen that day, balls of fluff running on long legs through the machair, their mum doing everything she could to distract us. We weren't a danger, but she was right to be wary. Better safe than sorry.

The chill didn't leave my back all that night. I tried rolling over, but my front tightened and the hairs on my head prickled. I was spooked, and only happy when the pink glow of dawn crept across the windows. Later Sue told us that the stables were haunted, that they hear horses come and go on summer evenings. They like to think they're horses from days gone by, just checking up on them.

DAY NINE
Benbecula to Grimsay

The ponies were breathtakingly handsome in the early light, heads high, nostrils fluted in velvety lines. A breeze lifted their manes and their foreheads gleamed. The trip was doing them good. They were alert and vital and in their element. We rode through the outskirts of Balivanich along quiet roads, we hoped to get to Grimsay before the day's traffic started up. We didn't fancy meeting buses on the North Ford (Oitir Mhòr) causeway, the five-mile loop of single-track road that links Benbecula and North Uist via the western tip of Grimsay. The sun climbed steadily ahead of us and brindled the sea with silver. On the skyline was Eabhal once again, and behind it the smaller but similarly shaped Burabhal – two ski-slope smiles canting to the west.

I looked back over my shoulder, with the sun behind us the colours were astonishingly lucid: Reeds gleamed gold, Cotton Grass flowers shone pearl white, two sheds boasted roofs of peacock green and teal blue. In his book *Hebridean Connection* Derek Cooper writes about the extraordinary light: 'I know few places in the world which have such an ability to improve on nature as in the Hebrides. It has something to do with ultra-violet rays, I'm told, but the intensity of the light, its magical powers of magnification and its aggrandisement of colour are to me unparalleled elsewhere.'

We passed a sign that read 'CAUTION: Otters Crossing' and rode onto the causeway. Ross was unsure, jumpy. The sea splashed forcefully against the causeway walls, and the incoming tide powered noisily through narrow channels beneath us. It was exhilarating, this walking over water with a fresh wind on our faces. A couple of work vans were approaching but we had plenty of time to trot to the next passing place. The drivers slowed, courteous and smiling. '*Failte gu Uibhist a Tuath*/ Welcome to North Uist', said a sign on the little island of Eileen na h-Airigh. Just one more stretch of causeway ahead and we'd be turning off to Grimsay.

'Car coming,' I shouted ahead to Shuna. We started trotting but I could hear the car coming up close and fast, I turned round and indicated to the driver to slow down. As we turned into a passing place he accelerated past us, a look of darkest anger on his face. 'Idiot,' I said to Shuna, inhaling exhaust fumes. I was shaken, feeling frayed with lack of sleep. I'd need to be careful today. Luckily Shuna was in a better humour than I.

We took the second turning signed for Grimsay and followed Catriona's instructions, and there she was, walking towards us and waving. We'd met her through long-distance riding. Like us she was passionate about getting out in the hills with her horse. She owned a house on Grimsay which she'd kindly offered us the use of. We'd be there alone as she and her husband were heading back to the mainland that morning. We followed a trail of Christmas tinsel that she'd thoughtfully tied onto fences and gateposts, 'in case you arrived after we left', she explained, to a field that belonged to her neighbour Theona. 'That's her house there,' she said, pointing to a white farmhouse built on a peninsula. The tide was in, and the house, surrounded by water, floated at the end of its slip of track. 'She's so excited about having the ponies to stay, very disappointed to miss you but she's away for a couple of days.'

Theona had left buckets filled with water in the field. I felt huge warmth for this woman and her welcoming water, her care, and her lovely name which I savoured quietly.

Back at the house we had breakfast with Catriona and her husband, Mike, a softly-spoken bushy-browed man who charmingly said 'touch wood' in almost every sentence. We were suddenly enfolded in a warm and organised world where every detail had been thought of. The instructions on how to leave the house were a masterpiece in attention to detail: 'leave the kettle empty and on its side'. I wanted to ask why but didn't, and felt so sloppy by comparison. Shame simmering again near my tired surface. I was self-conscious of our mucky, worn gear and ragged itinerary. Once alone Shuna and I sat in the upstairs living area looking over the garden of rhubarb and solar panels, to the tide now going out, the causeway, the stippled western horizon beyond.

I had a snooze then picked up *The Pebbles on the Beach* from the bookshelf. We'd hardly seen any shingle on our trip so far, in all these miles of sand. On Grimsay I was looking out at yet more sand, but this was grey and sludgy, the causeway was interfering with the old current patterns. I would be transported back to that place a few months later while reading about The North Ford in Terry J. Williams' book *Walking with Cattle*. While researching the book she was led across the sands on the same route they drove the cattle along on their way to the cattle sales in North Uist. She describes how a line of cairns had been built to mark the safe route across the ford:

'some kept their heads above water even at high tide. Most have disappeared, broken by storms, and scattered by the ever-meddling sea. Others are hardly distinguishable heaps, although a keen eye can still detect traces of the skill that made them. Every year the sea dislodged one more stone, widens one more crack. For now, enough remains for those who know to show those who don't how it used to be [...] in places there was a line of stones set in the sand like stepping stones between cairns [...] Angus showed me a remnant – one, two, three, four, each with its crown of seaweed – and I wondered how it felt to be not-quite-lost out here in darkness or swirling mist, trusting this thread of stones to lead you to the next cairn, listening for the sound of creeping water.'

In the early afternoon we set off with the ponies to explore Grimsay. We felt rested, and the beautiful day beckoned. We came to a field with a handful of tups, bachelor boys standing resting in the sun, one was a little way off from the others, head down he was well and truly caught up in wire. His flanks were heaving in the hot sun. We'd need wire cutters to set him free. When a pickup truck drove along towards us I lifted my arm and flagged it down. The woman driving wound down her window.

'Hi, there,' I said, smiling. 'Do you know who these sheep belong to?'

'Who's asking?' Her accent was surprising, American maybe.

'We're just riding through with ponies and saw there's a tup tangled in wire. I think he'll need cutting free.'

'Well, no doubt someone will be along.' With that she drove off, sour-faced. I felt my temper flare. What was her problem? Another car came along and stopped, a helpful woman called Joan, who it turned out lived in the house across the water from Catriona's, said she'd call the farmer straight away. When we came back later, we found the tup had been cut free.

The houses we rode by were immaculate. Lawns trimmed and mown, washing pegged precisely on tightly strung lines. 'It feels very sanitised here compared to Barra and South

Uist,' Shuna said. Later on a passer-by who stopped to pet the ponies explained it to us as being a 'religion thing': North of Benbecula is Presbyterian, South Uist and Barra are Catholic. 'You know how it goes,' she said cryptically. She added that there were a lot of incomers on Grimsay. You could understand why. This quintessentially picturesque 'stepping-stone island' with its stunning backdrop of Eabhal to the north, the sea all around, sheltered fishing harbours, tiny stone cottages, and its close proximity to the airport, was a little haven. 'Incomers', the word always landed somewhere difficult for me. I could never hear it without taking it a tiny bit personally, imagining there might be resentful undertones lurking. Sometimes there were, of course, but not always. All my life I'd lived as an incomer, my accent never fitting. That worn-out spool of conversation goes:

'Where are you from?'

'Scotland.'

'No, but where are you *really* from?'

I thought back to Anglesey. The first house Mum bought after she left Dad was a tumbledown farmhouse at the end of a long track. It was a freezing house with flagstone floors and no heating. We were troubled with what Mum called 'the prowler'. We never found out who it was but someone would walk around the house in the middle of the night. Mum borrowed a friend's dogs, two huge chow chows who would run around the inside of the house, barking and shadowing 'the prowler' as they made his or her sinister way around the outside. It was terrifying. After a few nights the prowler disappeared, but that sense of being an outsider, of being looked in on from the outside, of feeling vulnerable, never left me. Mum, being who she was, always outspoken and revelling in standing out (the only Mum at parents' evening to wear green contact lenses and a short ra-ra skirt) meant that we were always conspicuous in our difference. By contrast I loved going up to Oban to see Dad who was welcomed and respected in the community. I piggybacked on his belonging, loving that he had a clear role and that when I said who my father was people's faces softened. I loved that when I was with him 'normal' people would have me into their homes, give me tea and cakes, make a fuss.

We rode through the village of Bagh Mòr past the old stone pier, half on the lookout for Norman MacLean's house. Norman was a comedian, singer, poet and piper who Shuna remembered from ceilidhs in her family home years before. She'd just finished reading his autobiography *The Leper's Bell*. We didn't see a house that quite fitted the description we'd been given and weren't feeling up to knocking on doors. Pickup woman had dinted our confidence.

I'd seen Norman MacLean talking about 'creativity and values' on YouTube. He described himself as 'someone on the periphery of both societies, the English and the Gaelic, not quite belonging in either one'. It was strange for me to think of this legend in the Gaelic world as feeling that he didn't quite belong. Was it much more of an internal thing then, ultimately, to feel belonging? If you didn't feel like you fitted with yourself then it didn't matter how much Gaelic or heritage or connections to family or place you had. I wondered if that feeling of not quite belonging had been at the root of his alcoholism. He was living a sober life now.

A few months after we rode past his house he died, his obituary in the *Sunday Herald* told the story of how he'd been rescued by a teacher from Uist who'd found him in the Southern General hospital in Govan, and couldn't bear to see him die 'in some dingy flat , besieged by empties'. She'd said 'people in Uist love him and here we have a huge tolerance for drunks. Every family here has an alcoholic, so I knew he'd be safe.'

Beyond the village we stopped by a small hill loch. Its

almost-black surface was mottled with the claret leaves of Water Lilies. Two white flowers were just opening up, the first I'd seen this year. I'd read back at the Kildonan Museum that their rhizomes were used for dyeing Harris Tweed. They gave dark browns and black, but that it was dangerous harvesting. You had to walk in the loch barefoot and dig out the tenacious roots with your toes, people had drowned doing it. The rhizomes were also used for tanning leather out here in the Hebrides where trees were so scarce.

A farm vehicle pulled over. It was my daughter's school-friend Fergus and his father, Iain, both smiling out of the same long-lashed eyes.

'How is the revision going?' I asked Fergus.

'I'll be glad when it's all over!' They invited us to call round for a cup of tea later.

We carried on following signs for Kallin Shellfish Ltd. The car park was built on tons and tons of scallop shells. A convertible arrived at the same time as we did. Once again, I was taken back to Anglesey, and the throat-catching smell of scallop shells. I remembered one of Mum's boyfriends who'd taken me to Brownies in his convertible. I'd felt mortified by his shaved head, his strange car, and how the other Brownies peered out at us from the windows of Llanethli village hall. I only went once. Mum wasn't great at driving us to things. I can remember getting my hopes up about various clubs, activities. She'd take me to one maybe, and then the novelty would wear off. Perhaps the illness was working away in her even way back then. All those times she couldn't get us up for school, maybe she'd been ill our whole childhood.

'I'd imagined something smaller,' said Shuna. 'This is a factory.'

'Shall I hold the ponies and you go and have a look? If they've got sparkling water could you get me some?'

The ponies didn't want to stand still, possibly it was the smell of shellfish, or the clouds of dust lifting every time a vehicle came or went. Kallin Shellfish Ltd was a hive of activity, a booming business.

'What did you get?' I asked Shuna as she walked towards me holding a white plastic bag.

'Some squat lobsters, couldn't bring myself to buy scallops. They're all dredged, but got you some water.'

We decided to just go back the way we'd come. We were tired, dawn in Balivanich felt like a long time ago. I also had a peculiarly strong feeling of not wanting to let Eabhal out of sight, of wanting to stay facing north. On the way back we left the road where in the lee of a knoll we found a patch of sun-warmed rock. We sat down, looking west across Loch Hornaraigh, and beyond to the tidal channels around Catriona's house, which we could just make out. The ponies trailed their ropes and grazed between Bog Cotton stems. I walked to the tiny summit behind us where there was a tump, a pointed mound of turf about a foot high. Mussel shells were scattered around, and I imagined all the birds that stopped here to eat: Oystercatchers, Great Black-Backed Gulls, maybe birds of prey, their droppings fertilising the ground, building up over the decades, centuries even, into this green-topped nipple. Some people call them fairy hills. The bedrock around was covered in crusty black Lichens. There were Mosses too, red and yellow and frog green. Welts of bright white quartz ran through the gneiss. I knew exactly what to leave for Mum here. I dug about in the bead purse and found it, not a bead but an unpolished crystal shard, and lay it down on the rocks where it was absorbed by all the colours of that Lichen forest. Instant belonging!

I went back down and sat beside Shuna. We shared the Squat Lobsters and left the pink tail shells where we dropped them. Wriggling my toes inside my boots I looked across the loch to the hillside freckled with Hebridean Sheep. The best preserved Iron Age wheelhouse in the Uists was somewhere around here. We should explore, but the sun felt so good, and the ponies had stopped grazing and were resting. I thought of the lines from Pauline Prior-Pitt's poem *Late Adventure*: 'Lose control. Catch up with Vikings'. But once again we were too slow to catch up with anything, let alone Vikings, or early Celts. Then again maybe that's exactly what we had done, caught up with the ancient ones. There on that sun-warmed rock on Grim's Island sucking Shellfish through our teeth.

DAY TEN
Grimsay to North Uist

The ponies spun their bums to the wind as the rain struck. They were in the paddock in front of Bonnie View Croft at Carinish, owned by Heather and Ian Morrison. We'd been drinking tea and eating Penguin biscuits with them for the past hour or so, hearing about their own horses, their seven dogs. 'Rescues from Portree, Stornoway, South Uist.' They'd shown us their calves – Highlanders, Charolais crosses, a Limousin – and told us how they took in any orphaned calves on the Uists. It was obviously a labour of love, each one was named, were all finger-sucking friendly, had deep straw bedding, they even had Himalayan salt licks hanging from the gates. Before I could stop him, Ian, who was allergic to horses, had picked up my tack and carried it into the barn. That's who they were, through and through kind. Every creature on that place was loved and knew it.

We stepped under the Morrisons' porch overhang waiting for the rain squall to pass. The Morrisons had just left to go to the annual North Uist Tractor Rally. They'd encouraged us to attend, said that there'd be a great spread of cakes, and soup too. We said we'd try and make it along later.

'The weather's not great but at least there's a good bite of grass for them here,' Shuna said. Ross and Chief were dark with rain. We'd only ridden a few miles that morning, from Grimsay to Carinish in the south of North Uist. We were now waiting for Dorothy, Fergus's mum, who'd offered to drive us back to Iochdar to collect the pickup.

'This must be the last thing Dorothy needs on a Saturday morning,' I said to Shuna. She was a full-time teacher in Iochdar, and a very busy woman. We'd watched her car go past the house numerous times last night. Nonetheless she was smiling when we got in her car.

'I wish I was riding ponies for a few weeks,' she said. 'Getting away from the end of term madness. It's always hectic, but the Manchester bombing, those poor girls from Barra, well, it's hit everyone really hard. A lot of the children knew the girl who died, Eilidh, from the pipe band. They've decided to cancel the provincial Mòd next week.' Dorothy's words tumbled fast, full of feeling, as we drove back towards the North Ford Causeway, past the squat grey church we'd ridden past earlier with its algae-smeared 'For Sale' sign.

Dorothy pointed over to the shore on her left. 'That's the seaweed cutting there.'

I craned my neck.

'See, they're like circles on the surface of the water, that's what Iain does, he's a cutter, his father too. You harvest the Kelp when the tide's out, then put a rope around it in a circle. When the tide comes in it all lifts up, keeps it together until you're ready to sell it. There's a seaweed drying and processing plant on Uist. It's hard graft though,' Dorothy continued. 'Iain's got the perfect Hebridean build for it, a short back. You need to be very strong for that work.'

I was captivated by the image of the floating seaweed corrals. I'd never seen them before, nor even heard of them. I looked it up in my book *Flora Celtica* when I got home: 'Cutting the seaweed was the best work that ever came for the crofter because you had one week on and one week off, because of the tides.'

Like working for CalMac, I thought. The book continued to describe this centuries-old tradition:

> 'Teams of men worked down the beach with the receding tide, cutting the weed and throwing it behind them. As the tide turned they put a rope made from twisted heather stems around the floating mass, and at high tide pulled in the ropes and loaded their harvest onto hand barrows or carts. If working offshore, they towed it home behind the boat.'

We left the floating rope circles behind us as we drove across Benbecula, down through the water-drawn heart of it. Water, water everywhere. The mizzle was falling strongly now and we couldn't see Eabhal. Dorothy talked about this place, her life here, her family. She was a force, and I was full of admiration for her. There was a fierceness about her that made me want to duck low, to choose my words with care. A female Hen Harrier circled the land to our right, her banded tail spread wide. For a fleeting second I saw the fullness of her owly face. This place: strong birds, strong women, strong men. The Hen Harrier dissolved into the mist and I was left with a feeling of vertigo. We and the ponies were just clipping the edges of the circles-upon-circles of history and community and nature that lapped this place.

We stocked up at the Co-op in Benbecula and drove north, having reconnected once again with the pickup. We'd promised to pop in on Cubby and Anne who lived on North Uist, just east of Carinish. Driving over a carpet of Sea Thrift up the long track to their house, we saw the car and trailer parked outside. The cloud had lifted a little and we had 360° bird's-eye view for miles around, and there she was, Eabhal, back in sight. We knocked on the door and walked around the house but there was no sign of life. Another car arrived and a man approached. He was short as a child with a deeply lined face, a toothless grin.

'Are they in?' he asked, his eyes full of light, the bluest light.

'Well, they might be, but we can't raise them.'

Just then I saw a figure behind one of the windows.

'Did you see that?' I said. 'Looked like a person.'

Shuna shook her head.

'Aye,' said the man, 'I saw it too, maybe it was a ghost.' We knocked on the door again and this time Anne welcomed the three of us in.

Angus was a fisherman from Grimsay who had been helping Cubby with an uncooperative outboard motor. While they talked boats, Anne got a map out and showed us places to visit: Barpa Langas burial mound and Pobbal Fhinn stone circle just a few miles from where we were. I was struck again by Anne's voice. She spoke the Gaelic place names with her English accent, softly, clearly, roundly, owning every consonant and syllable. She talked about music, and the course she was studying in traditional music at the University of the Highlands and Islands. She also talked about starting up her own archaeological tours business. She was immersed in this place. No pretension, no changing her accent or muffling her words. She was who she was. Another map showed the island of Vallay where we were headed the next day. She pointed out where the standing stones and cup and ring markings were. 'And this place,' she said, pointing to Udal peninsula to the East of Vallay. 'It's something else. Make time to ride around it if you can.' She reeled off a list of its special interests, its wheelhouses and well.

We drank coffee and looked out on those south-west-facing views. There was a fledgling native tree plantation nearby. Cubby and Anne were keen to plant more themselves and to fence the sheep out. We told them we'd seen a dead lamb on the road at the Grimsay turning that morning, its mother grazing by its body. Cubby shook his head. 'Poor wee critter, the crofters put them on the roadside for the better grass, but ach, what a price to pay. The drivers are so fast. I won't even use a pushbike now, too dangerous. With the wind in your ears you can't hear vehicles approaching. Aye, what chance do the lambs have?' He went on to talk about his time working and living on Shetland. 'The animals were mad with hunger. They didn't clip the sheep up there, just pulled the wool.' He made a gesture with his hands. 'They were so starved the wool just came out.'

'Just pulled the wool,' repeated Angus.

Cubby went on to talk about the same Norman MacLean we'd thought about calling in on the day before on Grimsay. Cubby lived and worked on boats at one time, based out of Oban. He talked about one occasion when Norman had been on a bender and had spent four days on his boat.

'Every morning I'd give him his eggs. A West Coast man always has two eggs, by the way,' he said with a wink. 'So I'd give him his eggs and soldiers and a £20 note and off he'd go to the Claredon in Oban. After the fourth day my wife said I had to get rid of him. 'Either he goes or I go.' At that time my wife was my crew. We were due to head out to Tobermory the next day so I had a last go at him, trying to stop him going into the 'blue room', to use Norman's own words. He lost the rag: "Who the hell are you to be telling me what to do? You're in the premier fucking league yourself!"'

Before we left, I took screenshots of the sites Anne had circled in pencil on her maps.

'When you get to Vallay,' said Cubby, as we said our goodbyes, 'go directly north across the island. There's a bay there, a beautiful spot, and there are always ducks on the sea. If you approach carefully, you'll see them. Mind to look out for those ducks.'

We drove north again, past Chief and Ross standing in their field. They looked up, recognising the sound of the pickup. 'I'm feeling bad for them in that rain,' said Shuna. 'It'll be nice to give them a feed later. Did you soak some speedibeet?' I nodded. We drove through sheets of rain, the windscreen wipers swiping drops across the views of lochans and low black cloud.

'I think we turn right here,' I said, seeing a sign for Barpa Langass. We parked in the car park. It seemed like the first place we'd been to that was properly set up for visitors, with signage and a good path. We put on our waterproofs inside the cab as it was blowing a proper hoolie outside. Past the kissing gate was an information panel, the cairn we could see on the skyline, a pile of grey stone through the rain, 'was about five thousand years old, a chambered cairn built by Neolithic farmers, a great mass of stone which would have dominated the surrounding landscape with a relatively small burial chamber inside'.

It also told us that five thousand years ago the landscape would have been covered in woodland before the spreading of the blanket peat.

Walking heads down, hoods up, over the smooth heather-dark hillside towards the pile of stones described in Alec Finlay and Ken Cockburn's book *the road north*: 'after a mound of time/ the pickle of boulders/is still sound'. Unfortunately we couldn't go inside where the poets had sensed the dark 'as a membrane/ of time'. We'd take their word for it. Time was doing its thing, moving on, and now it was deemed unsafe to enter the cairn. We peered through a metal grill, busy imagining, as rain ran across the backs of our hands.

Back in the steamy pickup we continued down the road to Poball Fhinn Stone Circle. It felt a little less well-trodden here as we moved aside pink Dog Roses that claimed the path. They were heavy with rain and the scent was intense. Walking in silence along the little path that led to the stone circle, we drifted apart on our own urges. Shuna walked uphill into the mist and I stayed put. Rain blurred my sight and my eyelashes flickered against my hood like heartbeats.

Mum would have loved this place.

Mum would definitely have come to this place.

Mum must have been here.

This is so Mum.

I felt in my pocket for the bead purse, not there. Tears surfaced. It must be back with the saddlebags and ponies. I bent down and picked a tuft of Cotton Grass, and a pink flower which I looked up later, Heath Milkwort, and laid them both across the top of the stone that had most drawn me. It was cleaved into three, like those trees that begin as three and grow together, their trunks melding into one over time. The rock was like that, individuating but collaborating. The flowers lay bright in a fold of stone. I touched the Bog Cotton, silky soft, and picked another two, *one for each of your children, Mum. You said you'd have had more children if you hadn't got sterilised. Funny to imagine you like that, maternal.*

I looked over Loch Langais to the south, remembering a holiday in France. I couldn't sleep for hearing Mum and Paul 'making babies' as they called it, the noises had terrified me. I knocked on the door and said, 'Please can you stop that noise.' Paul had looked round, eyes strange and huge with his glasses off. 'We're allowed our fucking fun too,' he'd shouted.

That same holiday I'd bent down to kiss Mum goodnight. She was reading in bed and lifted her head up at the same time, crack, the blaze of her pain, my shame. 'I think you've broken my nose.' I'd hurt her when all I'd wanted was to give her love. She maintained her nose was never the same again.

The rain wasn't letting up. Still no sign of Shuna. I was suddenly missing her intensely, but soon she reappeared out of the mist and joined me amongst the standing stones. There, in the waist-high Heather, was the softest brush of pale green. The

Willow was flourishing in the shelter of the Heather, keeping a low profile amongst the fallen stones. Growing so green, so surprising. Willow, 'seileach' in Gaelic. Each letters in the Gaelic alphabet was traditionally associated with a native tree, in one version seileach represents the 's'. I plucked the end from a delicate branch and laid it against the flowers I'd put in the hold of that stone. *There, Mum. You'd like that. S for sex.*

The sky was lower than ever as we drove over the causeway onto the island of Baleshare where we would spend the night with Shuna's friend Anna-Wendy. Following her precise directions, counting down gates and cattlegrids, a schoolhouse and a caravan, we reached her house. By now we were soaked through. She showed us the drying room, invited us to have a hot bath. It was perfect.

The house was filled with musical instruments. A bright yellow trombone caught my eye. Both Anna-Wendy and her husband, Simon, were professional musicians. She was the Programme Leader for the applied music degree at the University of the Highlands and Islands. I loved listening to her talking about falling in love with this place, about the view from the plane flying in. 'This place is mostly water, you know.' Her skin shone as her words gave shape to her life there. 'I love that hill,' she said, nodding towards Eabhal. 'I love being able to look out at it every day.'

That evening Anna-Wendy had an exhibition opening at Taigh Chearsabhagh Arts Centre in Lochmaddy. Shuna and I needed to find somewhere to leave the pickup and trailer near the island of Vallay. We arranged to drive across and find a spot to leave it, and for Anna-Wendy to pick us up on her way home. We drove slowly up and over the Committee Road. This straight road through the heart of North Uist to the village of Sollas, opposite the island of Vallay, was organised by a committee charged with providing famine relief in the 1840s. Building it was a way to give people a wage. We topped the highest point on the road and descended alongside a commercial pine forest that stretched down to the shore where the tide was well in. Vallay sat across the water. We drove along the road past a few scattered houses. There was little sign of life, it was late, and I had a feeling of wanting to disappear, to not ask any more favours of anybody. We were listening to the first track on *Far Flung Collective*, lyrics written by Alex Roberts and a CD Anna-Wendy had collaborated on:

> *A small world indeed*
> *and it begins at your door*
> *the middle of nowhere*
> *and the centre of all*

There were a couple of building plots for sale. We stopped and saw a phone number written on the 'For Sale' sign. 'We could try giving them a call and see if they'd mind us parking the horsebox there for a couple of nights,' I suggested. Shuna volunteered to make the call, and while she wandered off to get phone signal, I looked across to Vallay, listening to the rest of the song:

> *dots, specks of land*
> *remote and unknown*
> *and far-flung and far-fetched*
> *and far too far from home*
> *but listen but listen if you have ears to see*
> *this tune's from a small world*
> *a small world indeed*

Shuna opened the door. 'They sound lovely, Angus and his partner Kathryn. They live just along there, a new house in the trees. She has horses and we can leave the box there. We're to go along now. Heh, maybe she'll want to ride with us tomorrow.'

As we turned back onto the road a Short Eared Owl flew alongside us, skimming the Pine-tops with the last of the late light.

DAY ELEVEN
Carinish to Vallay

It was Sunday. At home that's the only day we'd choose to ride out on main roads; no wood-wagons or delivery vans, and a lot fewer cars. But here on North Uist the cars kept coming. We were in the middle of church rush hour, going both ways it seemed. Southwards to the Free Church of Scotland in Carinish, and northwards, in the same direction as we were riding, to the Church of Scotland in Clachan. When we got to the church the car park outside was packed with more vehicles in one place than we'd seen since leaving Oban. A broad man was attending at the church entrance. He smiled at us, and an inquisitive part of me would have liked to have tied up the ponies and joined the service. We waved as we passed and a body of churchgoers cheerily waved back.

We trotted along the main road making good time, turning off the A865 onto the single-track Committee Road before the wave of after-church traffic started. We got off the ponies and walked, I took off my hi-vis jacket and stuffed it into a saddlebag. Just then a police car came up behind us and I had my customary gut-jolt of guilty conscience, but the car slowly drove past. What a day! The sun was shining and everything was lucent and sharp-edged compared to the rain-slurred dimness of the day before.

After stopping by a grassy gateway to let the ponies graze, I sat on the verge looking through the gate, its rungs sawn through with rust, meeting like ill-knitted bones. Strands of wool hung on the fence wire. This was the tup park, where a group of half a dozen, a mixture of deep-horned blackfaces and oval-eared cheviots, gazed at us with interest. Behind them, lifting over the flatness of the peat moor to the south, was Eabhal.

'Feels like it might be lunchtime,' Shuna said, mirroring my thoughts.

'How about we go to the standing stone and stop for lunch?' The stone on the skyline leaned heavily to the east above where the road curved away beneath the contour lines of Beinn á Charra. Back on the ponies we followed the road. It felt strange to be travelling in such a straight line.

The road was open to the moor on both sides, rectangles where peat had been cut in previous years were a-quiver with bog cotton, and peaty pools shone between. We left the road at the end of the straights, walked through a gate and headed up the hillside. The ground here had clearly been improved over the years. Between the patches of rushes was good dry pasture, but I was aiming straight for the stone on the skyline. A group of Blackface Ewes appeared beside it and only then did I see the scale of the standing stone, it was huge, over nine feet tall. We heard later that it had been put there to look like a human figure on the hillside, the idea being that invading Vikings would have been so horrified by the size of the locals that they'd have turned their boats and gone elsewhere to maraud.

'You'd never know it was this big unless you walked up here,' said Shuna, resting back against the broad lean of the stone's body. On the grass we picnicked on oatcakes and a tin of 'Filets de Maquereaux à la Moutarde'. A breeze blew warm on our faces and the air trembled with the sorcerous call of a Curlew. What a magical place. The stone is known in Gaelic as Clach

Bharnach Bhraodag, (limpet stone of Freya), Freya being the Norse goddess of love and beauty, and it dwarfed the ponies as they grazed. The Committee Road glinted like a seam of quartz through the flat peat moors below. My eyes picked out the white boxy shape of a Transit Luton van beetling along, taking me back to another van, on a day as dreich as today was sunny.

After Mum died neither Will nor Tom nor I had the heart to empty her flat, but Will finally forced the issue by emptying its contents into a Luton van. The flat had never belonged to her. It belonged to Will, and now he was renting it out for holiday lets and needed it emptying. The van was also his, and it was going out on hire the next day. So, we just had to get on with it, this sorting out of her stuff.

The Luton was bright white and had an electric tail lift. We'd moved it into his shed and it dripped onto the swept concrete while rain slated the steel roof overhead. We'd stood back, the three of us. There's this three-thing coming down the maternal line, two brothers and a sister. Like Mum I have two brothers, like me my daughter has two brothers. When my daughter was born Mum said, 'I'm so happy for you, it's lovely to have a girl.' I was ecstatic to have my baby girl, but remember my questioning her words. *Did she really mean that?* Her relationship with her own mum, as far as I could tell, had been completely messed up, as was her mother's with her mother, and us, well, it wasn't easy, hadn't been easy for a long time. A lot had happened since my daughter's birth and the van-emptying day though, and, I saw things differently. Now, almost two decades later, I could hear the authenticity in her words.

I hadn't known exactly what was in the van, but I was sure there'd be lots of books. Just thinking of them had lodged a shard of sorrow in my throat. It was the books I'd buckle under. Will pushed up the sliding door and there it all was, Mum's stuff. I had to turn away as the air from the van reached me, bringing a wave of Mum-ness with it. I missed her. I could smell her. My brain knew it wasn't her, just a load of stuff, but the rest of me didn't. The animal sensing reaching-out parts of me didn't.

We'd started to move things around. Her treasures: Afghan donkey-paniers, meticulously embroidered with silk, pieces of antique pottery, a specimen of a huge centipede, stretched out behind glass, a jar brimful with iridescent Scarob Beetles, and the beads, drawers and boxes and packets and pouches full of them, her passion. Seemingly she'd never had two pennies to rub together, but we were standing in the middle of Aladdin's Luton. She'd been a collector, she'd had insatiable appetites, not only for beads but for 'culture', for treasure, for travel, for men.

'So much stuff,' I said out loud. A paperback caught my eye, a picture of a full-mouthed, dainty-nosed little girl, her long hair pulled back, *Frost in May*. I picked it up and turned it over: 'Set in the Convent of the Five Wounds…a lyrical account of the death of a soul…' The girl on the cover looked uncannily like that tiny square black-and-white photograph I'd seen of Mum, pretty and pale and under-the-smile sad. I remember her telling me about being sent off to a convent when she was seven, how she was always hungry, how she'd never had enough of anything. So maybe that's why she collected stuff.

I picked up a doll's head, it was life-size and made of ebony-coloured porcelain. The neck gaped where there had once been a body attached, and inside the hollow was a mechanism. I held it up towards the light to get a closer look. The eyelashes slid up and two chestnut-brown eyes looked directly down into my own.

Lying in another open drawer of books was a jotter, the yellow cover sprouted green polka dots and a crocodile playing a game of pool. I opened it, a continental exercise book with tiny squares. On the front page Mum's handwriting said, *Morocco 1997 with Moira.* I flicked to another page: *his hands off me. Slimeball with bad temper. Thought it was Christmas. He was talking to me and stroking his cock.* I flicked to the previous page, wanting to know who she was talking about: *Well, the 'auberge' couldn't be more 'simple'... Bare room with 3 pallets in it. Clean lavatories – nowhere to wash our bodies. The manager takes the biscuit. Nasty piece of work. Had to tell him to take...* I read it out to the boys. 'No waaaay.' Tom laughed. 'That was Mum for you.' He knew better than any of us having travelled to Morocco with her, and Afghanistan, and Pakistan. Africa too. 'A nightmare', he'd said, but he's got a big heart. So has Will. They'd both been able to stretch into being with Mum, whereas I had shrunk from it.

Taking a deep breath I stretched my arms wide by the big-person stone there on North Uist, remembering the line in *Braveheart*, something about the standing stones making men hard and women fertile. I smiled. I knew what I'd leave in this place: clasps Mum had brought back from Morocco. There were three in the purse, one lapis, one jade, one jet, all set in silver. I'd splash out, leave all of them here. I got a toehold on the rock and tried to climb but my nerve failed me. There was a ridge on the rock that I could reach with my fingertips, I placed the clasps there, one two three, side by side. As I jumped down a tuft of Lichen brushed my hand. I found a small round glass bead, the colour of milky sapphire, and placed it on the celadon Lichen. I took a photograph lest I forgot just how beautiful it was, that bead nestled on the Lichen on the leaning stone.

Going through the gate back onto the Committee Road I noticed the gatepost was hollowed out at the top. Inside was a collection of pebbles, and further down the post was a hole where the wood had rotted away. Somebody, I presumed a person, had placed a smooth round red pebble inside. It felt nice to be in the footsteps of a fellow leaver of treasure. As we walked slowly up the tarmac hill, rows of hand-cut peats radiated outwards on either side. The ditches from which they'd been taken shone dark and treacly, the vertical cut-marks a running tally of hard graft. The peats were laid out to dry in rows of four, others were stacked in tipi shapes, their edges turning lighter as they dried. Wooden posts, written on with thick black permanent marker, laid claim to each crofter's peats: 'DONALD JOHN' from 'MONACH VIEW' had made a particularly tidy job of his.

The road topped the highest point and dropped down gently towards the north coast of the island where an old tractor was sinking slowly into the peat. Nearby was a metal plaque on a stone telling the tractor's story: *TEF-20/Artist Liz Crichton 2015/The TEF-20 tractor transformed crofting practices on Uist. Bought originally to work on one of the Knockintoran crofts, it now lies abandoned where it was last used. The non-functional engine covers having been discarded, and with a seat made from a recycled plastic box, it is slowly oxidising, gradually returning to the earth from which the ore was once mined. The hues of its rusty iron and rubber reflect the colours of the peat bog and heather on which it sits where it has become part of this landscape.*

I liked that the artist had identified it as a work of art, which is my own response when I come across old tractors listing to the earth they once worked. Its contemporaries and successors had been out in force yesterday at the tractor rally, most of them lovingly restored and now kept indoors. Others, like this one, were slowly turning to tractor skeletons and sinking into the sinewy world of peat. I wondered about other skeletons too, of all the Horses and Ponies that had worked these islands through the centuries, where all their bones were lying. Were some under us right now, slowly feeding calcium back into the acidic ground? I put my hand out, touched Ross's shoulder, and was glad, as ever, of his sturdy warmth beside me. How I loved him.

At low tide we rode out to Vallay across wet sand. Ross and Chief were excited to have company. Akiko, Kathryn's Warmblood mare, was in high spirits and happy to show off her elegant moves. Kathryn rode her beautifully, they made a stunning pair. Chief and Ross were carrying everything we'd need for the night: food, tent, sleeping bags. We were also carrying water as we'd been told finding drinking water might be a problem. As we got nearer the island the deserted buildings came into sharp focus: gable ends drawn on a bright blue sky where once there had been roofs.

'If you like, I can show you where I quite often ride on Vallay. There should be plenty of time before the tide comes back in,' Kathryn said. We both nodded, delighted to have a guide. As we left the beach we could hear Corncrakes rasping in the fields and I remembered Fiona MacRae, a friend back home, warning me not to camp this side of the island, that the Corncrakes had driven her to distraction all night long.

A very grand gatepost, round with a turret shape at the top, seemed to mark the place where sea handed over to land. There was no sign of its partner, long since claimed by the tides. We left the stone-built house and farm steadings behind and rode to the north side across cattle-poached marshland bright with King Cups and Early Marsh Orchids. Soon we reached a crescent of golden sand scooping around seaweed-flanked skerries. Out beyond the rocks were Cubby's ducks, now lifting off the water in a fuss of sun-wrought silver. Shuna and I caught each other's eye and smiled.

'This is a great spot to camp,' Kathryn said. 'You can watch the sun go down over the sea.' We got off the ponies and undid the saddlebags, unstrapped the tent, left everything in a pile above Tràigh Shimìlih. Then we followed Kathryn and Akiko west through the dunes to the next sandy bay. A smell of cucumber, strong and fresh and sweet, followed, and I wondered if it was algae of some sort. Akiko hunkered down on her haunches and slid down the dunes, walked into the sea up to her belly, brave and at ease in her environment. Meanwhile it took a lot of persuasion to get Ross and Chief past the white wavelets at the tideline. Then when we got into deeper water they spooked as the waves slapped their stomachs and rushed ashore. We all laughed. Leaving the beaches we rode through grassland towards the west end of the island, the ponies started tossing their heads and sneezing. 'Must be the pollen from all that clover,' Shuna said. It felt like we'd been spirited to the land of milk and honey.

The ponies spotted the Highland stirks before we did and halted. Heads lifted, stock-still, they stared at a herd of about thirty young Highlanders, horns shining amongst a mixture of cream and dun and red Cattle. When they saw us, they drifted towards us, slowly at first, then a few broke into a loose trot.

'Let's just walk quietly down here, out of sight,' said Kathryn, pointing towards the beach on the south side of the island. 'If we go out of sight they're bound to get bored.'

The ponies felt electric. There is nothing like a potential stampede to stir up a flight animal, but the stirks lost interest, and we sedately followed the bays that scalloped their way back towards the farm buildings.

'That looks like Angus,' said Kathryn, 'coming to check the cows.' She was pointing to a vehicle driving across the sand from North Uist. Shuna had been in touch with Angus MacDonald, who owned Vallay, months before. He'd been very welcoming, encouraging us to come and camp with the ponies.

The midnight blue Mitsubishi came to halt in front of us and Angus stepped out smiling, shirt sleeves rolled up.

'Ah, so you've made it,' he said, eying up the ponies, 'and it's yourself, Kathryn, your horse will be glad of having the company to ride out with.'

After a few minutes of chatting Kathryn said, 'I'd better be going then, before this tide comes in. Have a great night, and get in touch tomorrow. Maybe we could ride round Udal.' She pointed to the peninsula that Anne had told us so much about. 'I'm up for it if you are,' she added, 'and remember to take care with the tides tomorrow. Don't leave it too late. When it comes in it comes in fast!'

With that she and Akiko trotted off and it seemed mere seconds had passed before they were tiny in the distance.

'I see her out on the horse, but I've never actually spoken to her. Can you believe that?' he said, shaking his head. 'I've known her boyfriend, Angus, his whole life. Beautiful horse she's got there.'

'How come you're so keen on the horses and so welcoming?' asked Shuna. 'That's very unusual for a farmer nowadays.'

'I like the horses. And my daughter, she loves horses, that's what she works at, away down in England. You could say she's educated me. And I like to see people enjoying the place. Come on, and I'll walk up with you and show you where the water is.'

As we walked back towards the roofless farmhouse he pointed out the old cottages over on our right, and the walled enclosures that he used as cattle pens. 'Two hundred cattle I have out here, you know. Great cattle land. They're all pedigree Highlands. A lot go to Germany and Denmark. I cut all the silage here, got so much last year I've a heap left over to finish off this year. It's a fertile place this.' He explained how he and

143

his wife, Michelle, had recently bought Vallay after farming it as tenants for fourteen years.

'I love this place. Even though I've bought all this land, I'm still a crofter at heart. I want people to enjoy it. Someday I'll do up the houses. I trained as an agricultural engineer and worked on civil engineering projects in the Uist.' He paused. 'But I'm a crofter, that's what I am.'

By now we'd reached the farm steadings. We could see that some of the buildings had recently been re-roofed in aluminium. 'Here's a good stone trough, plenty of clean water,' Angus said. Ross sank his nose in, taking a long drink, and I realised with a pang of conscience that he'd not had fresh water all day. We untacked the ponies and let them wander off, spoilt for choice in a land of plenty. I topped up my water bottle, drinking water wouldn't be problem after all.

'It's many years since we last used that,' Angus said, nodding towards a steep-sided sheep dip. 'There used to be sixty people living here. The steading was built in the sixteen hundreds. At one time that was the farm manager's house.' He pointed towards the house we'd passed. 'There was also a schoolhouse, a butchery, dairy, smithy. Look, there's the pigsties. Aye, this place had it all. Later, much later of course, there was the big house built up there, Vallay House, built in the early nineteen hundreds.' Set away from all the other buildings it sat alone on the skyline, a shell emptied of all its grandeur but still telling a story.

'That was some place in its day,' Angus added. Our imaginations travelled back through time. Snipe drummed over the marshland nearby. 'We lost a daughter, you know,' he said. He told us about Ellie who had died of cancer while she was at university, her indomitable character, her positivity right to the end. How much she'd have wanted something good to have come out of it all. 'That's why we started "One Million Miles for Ellie". Have you seen it on Facebook?' We shook our heads, both of us making a mental note to donate. 'I'd better be getting back ahead of that tide. My mother will be out tomorrow to check the cows, keep a look out for her.'

He walked back to his truck carrying his and Michelle's loss, the barely imaginable agony of losing a child.

We placed the saddles inside the doorway of the old farm manager's house. 'Just in case it rains,' Shuna said. A Starling arrived with a beak full of tiny Worms. She perched on a wall nearby before flitting towards us. We were clearly in her entranceway. *Dare I, daren't I*, she seemed to be saying. She flitted off, she daren't. Her nestlings were too precious to risk betraying their whereabouts.

The tent was up, mats inflated, sleeping bags laid out. We'd eaten delicious soup made with noodles and fish, Tabasco and miso. We put more wood on the fire, wood that we'd collected back at the steadings that had been discarded when they re-roofed the sheds. I picked up the half-bottle of *Jura Superstition* and poured another peaty dram. The north-westerly breeze lifted ash and smoke from the fire. Gulls called as they fed off the sea coming in over the warm sand. In the furthest distance we could see St Kilda, a small cone of mauve enticing on the horizon. The tide was coming closer, waves slapped noisily against the skerries. I rubbed my hands, still damp and chilled from when I'd gone down to the sea to wash the cooking pots. The water had felt deceptively warm in comparison to the dropping air temperature. The sun was sinking in an orange glow behind slivers of cloud. Seagulls began to drop down onto the shore, crying their bedtime banter.

'It's after ten,' said Shuna. 'Shall we walk out to the point to watch the last of the sunset?' Across the machair Primroses glowed like lemony stars. As we headed over the rocks to the point we disturbed a lone Goose, who took off and landed splashily on the sea. A Seal rolled roundly alongside him. We sat down, rocks apart, lost in our own thoughts. I brushed my hand across the Sea Pinks next to me, petals Rizla-dry against my palm. On the turning tide the gull chatter quietened. The sun burned a dent in the sea and slowly dropped into it.

Walking back to the tent, our faces and fingers stiff with cold, three Fairy Terns flew by, their tails ribboning through the plaited sundown sky.

DAY TWELVE
Leaving Vallay

Shuna was moving about outside the tent.

'Morning, what time is it?' I asked.

'Half eight,' she replied. 'I had a text from Kathryn, sent at midnight, saying she hoped we were watching the sunset, the best she's ever seen here. Beady, I think we may have gone to bed before the party started!'

'But we saw the sun go down.'

'Yeah, but the colour show must have started after that. I did wonder,' she added, 'when I went out at 4am for a pee the horizon was on fire. Really sweet, Kathryn's invited us to stay with her tonight, rain's forecast. She's on her own, Angus is away working.'

We'd talked about staying two nights on Vallay, but if rain was coming in it would be a treat to be in a house, and last night had been so perfect, it would be hard to beat.

The three Terns from last night skittered by, all pointed wings and forked tails and chattering noisily, so close I could make out the flash of orange on their beaks, the tiny stab of black at the tip. I stood up and headed to the shore, crossing the sand to the huddle of rocks covered in seaweed. When I put my hand down to steady myself Bladderwrack slipped under my palm. Looking closer at the fronds of seaweed, on each one a mid-rib was visible and decorated with air sacks like small green olives. Oystercatchers pipped at me while I watched a canary-yellow Sea Snail take close-in suckery steps, stretch by shiny stretch. The magic of being down on this level, how much we miss as our heads go about our days all the way up there in the air, so far away from our feet.

I stepped onto the body of dry rock, where clumps of Sea Pinks seasoned the stone, and walked carefully to the end where it met a milky sea. It was a clouded-over day and St Kilda was nowhere to be seen. The rock I was standing on was black, marked with splashes of dove-grey and old-gold Lichen. I would leave the pottery fish bead here on the rocks, and the next spring tide would draw it away. A friend of Mum's in Galloway had made these pottery fishes for her thirty years previously. Mum tended to stay clear of 'craft', seeing what she did as 'art', but this little pottery fish, with its blobby gold spots and clumsy yellow outline, was surely craft, and had somehow slipped through the net. I squatted down, laying it on the rock, and yes, it belonged. Its spots were the same colour as the Lichen, its body the very same green-brown as the Bladderwrack below.

Mum hadn't been a great one for exercise, and was scornful of 'sporty' people, but she liked going for walks and riding. She also liked to swim. Some of my earliest memories are of her swimming in the public pool in Holyhead. I can still feel the surges of her strong breaststroke, how dizzily dangerous it had felt clinging on to her shoulders. Dad has a cine film of us in Ghana. Mum, young and slim, flared trousers, midriff showing and her hair swinging impossibly thick and red. A barrage of hair, surely too much for one person. And that colour, bright bay if she'd been a horse. The film, silent and speeded up, of her under a tree smoking a cigarette, walking and joking with the Ghanaian grooms at a polo yard, us being given pony rides. The African bush and the old Cortina on red dirt roads. Dad, young and handsome, his beard dark, eyes smiling. Will's face already full of mischief, Tom and I white-blonde from the sun. The three of us splashing in an outdoor swimming pool, playing and performing for the camera. Mum at the side of the pool, laughing, diving in. I touched the pottery fish bead one last time. If I had another, I would have left it here, nose to tail with this one, like her star sign, Pisces.

Mum's favourite bird, the Raven, croaked as we approached Vallay House which sat eerily in the muted morning light. I couldn't see the bird, but the ponies were on the skyline by the house, heads up, looking straight at us. Ross's mane was lifting out in all directions. He was getting saltier and wilder-looking by the day. They were standing against the disarray of an old iron fence, each upright post leaning waywardly, each cross-piece unsprung, a far cry from the neat line it must once have been. The rufous red of its rust stood out against the wet pigeon colour of the house walls. Gold Lichen swept the house's graceful lines and curves. Large square windows, and small porthole-shaped ones, looked out at us, lacklustre without glass. The crow-stepped gable ends bit into a dull sky.

Parked outside the house was a tractor, rusted away to finger-touch crumble. The sea air had been hard on it. We looked through windows and saw tiled fireplaces, moulded ceilings fallen to the floor, a fire grate in mid-air where the first floor had collapsed. A sister Starling to the one we'd seen yesterday landed on the grate, hissing, her mouth full of Grubs, before hopping up into the chimney cavity.

'Do you know anything about this place?' I asked Shuna. 'Did someone say it belonged to a photographer?'

'Yes, a historian and photographer, his name was Erskine Beveridge.'

'What a great name.'

'It's a sad story. His son inherited the house and lived here alone. He was forbidden from marrying the love of his life, became an alcoholic and died crossing the sands to Vallay, caught by the tide.'

The Raven croaked again. So close now it must have been somewhere in the building. Maybe it had a nest here, or was just on the prowl. We looked in on a circular room as a Pigeon flew low over the fallen debris following the curve of the wall, soft feather-flap of air as it passed before disappearing through an archway. The place was derelict but pulsing with life.

Ross and Chief followed us back down to the steading. 'We'll be back for you soon,' I said to them, climbing over a wall. We wanted to explore the east end of the island and Angus had asked us not to go with the ponies as there were cows calving. As Shuna climbed over the wall beside me a buff bird whirred by before disappearing into the long grass.

'A Corncrake!'

'That's the first one I've ever seen,' said Shuna. 'Oh, this place...' I couldn't agree more.

The tide was going out and we followed a trail of neat cattle hoof-prints and tiny pink cockle shells across the bay towards the promontory of Àird Mhic Caoilt. Past a gate with a hand-painted sign warning Cows Calving, Please Keep Out were the dun and the standing stones that Anne had told us about. The dun was easy to spot, a circular stone-built wall straddling the pre-existing bedrock. The sea was encroaching now, and I wondered how it had looked when it was first built

3,000 years or so ago. Had there been trees, and where had the high tide mark been way back then? Now the tides were breathing on the dun and sometime in the not-too-distant future the sea would take it. We sat on the grassy top of the wall but weren't the only ones to ever rest there. Little tubes of goose shit were dotted all about. There was a fence running through the middle of the dun with seaweed hanging from each square of rylock. I loved that this fence was there, that there were no paths to this ancient site, no signage, and wham-bam, a stock fence put up right through its centre. It was a living, breathing monument with tides and Cattle and Geese smoothing its edges.

There was an entrance way to the right, a beautifully crafted stonework channel that I imagined had originally been a doorway but was now a conduit for the sea. A tiny bird watched us from a grass tump beyond the dun. Bright glare from the sun came through the cloud and the air was warm. To my left a thick hessian rope dropped from beneath the turf, hanging over the inner wall of the dun and disappearing into a tangle of seaweed and silverweed below. I found my bead, a gemstone I didn't know the name of. Roughly shaped, its purple hues picked up the blush of an empty crab's shell and the pink in the quartz running through the gneiss. I threaded the bead and tied it onto the thick rope, drawing the knot extra tightly.

'Shall we leave the standing stones for another day?' Shuna said. 'It's so nice just sitting here, listening to the Oystercatchers.' I nodded, feeling a jolt of pleasure at the thought of coming back here sometime.

A quiet while later we left the dun and headed back towards the waiting ponies. The Highland stirks from yesterday were this side of the island now, it must have been their prints we'd seen earlier. They followed us, halting when we stopped to look

153

back at them, their coats rippling like reeds in the breeze, eyes hidden by forelocks. Between us and them horn-tipped shadows glistening on the sand.

We left Vallay the way we'd come, past the turreted gate post. Beyond it was its missing partner, recumbent in the rocks but visible from this angle. I got off Ross to take a closer look. Bricks radiated out from the centre of its upturned base like petals of a flower. P & M HURLL GLASGOW said each rosy rectangle.

We dropped off our gear at the pickup outside Kathryn and Angus's house, and leaving the ponies to stand in the newly built loose boxes, went inside for a cup of tea.

'Can't believe you went to bed last night.' Kathryn laughed. 'Angus and I sat upstairs for hours watching the sky. It was a blaze of pinks and oranges, well after midnight. We thought you two must have been flipping out. It must be the best sunset we've ever seen here!'

Later, after an exhilarating gallop across the strand to Solas and Angus's parents' croft, Kathryn picked us up and we drove down to the shore.

'We need to hurry,' she said, 'cockling on the rising tide is not the easiest. Hopefully we're not too late.' We took off our boots and socks and Kathryn showed us how to look for the little tufts of Algae which were the telltale signs of Cockles. Her technique was to dig in with a fork and pop them out. It was a blissfully meditative task. Our feet got cold as Kathryn's Labrador Darrach guddled happily nearby. Soon the green plastic basket was heavy with shellfish.

That night we feasted on cockles and spaghetti, the Prosecco was flowing as we looked across the treetops to Vallay through an entire wall of glass. Kathryn showed us architect drawings of the beautiful cabins they were planning to build in their forest retreat. We talked Owls and Eagles, Horses and previous lives. It turned out Kathryn had done her Assistant Riding Instructor training at Gleneagles at around the same time as Shuna. Although they'd never met, they'd heard of each other, knew the same people and the same horses. I went to bed tipsy, revelling in the sense of what a small world it was, and that there were surely Short Eared Owls roosting close by in the Sedges.

DAY THIRTEEN

Solas to Berneray

'Look at the swans,' I said.

Shuna slowed the pickup to a standstill and we watched, through a rainy windscreen, a family of Mute Swans, two parents and six cygnets, cross the road in front of us. They were walking from Loch Aonghais on the right down to the shore on our left. From the nursery to the sea. Wind ruffled the cygnets' baby down and their heads, the size of cockle shells, had halos of silver. Six little scrappy angels, focusing intently on their feet, on following.

We carried on, soon catching up with Kathryn. We were following her to the island of Berneray where we'd leave the pickup and horsebox at the ferry terminal, and get a lift with her to Lochmaddy, the main town in the Uists. We were keen to visit the arts centre there, Taigh Chearsabhagh.

The exhibition was called 'THE LOBSTER AND THE LACUNA/An Giomach agus an Fhaochag'. Its blurb said: *A new exhibition takes us on a descent through the logbooks of Roberta Sinclair, naturalist and submariner. Her entries offer a glimpse into the 1950s heyday of the Hebridean Cable Transit company, and its underwater exploration of the Sound of Harris.*' It gave a definition of '*Lacuna*' – *a genus of small inter-tidal mollusc; A gap or vacancy; A prolonged silence; A missing piece of text or information.*

I was captivated by the exhibition: the life-size model of Roberta's submersible 'Effie' where you could feel the vibrations and hear the sounds she would have experienced under the sea. Roberta's logbook entries had been reproduced on the walls:

1st July 1957. I am standing on the shore at Bays Loch, looking down the Grey Horse Channel towards Hermetray. My conveyance, car No 72 of the Hebridean Cable Company, hangs next to me in her newly modified form. The air smells of seaweed, pitch and diesel smoke.

5th May 1957. I have renamed Effie 'The Lacuna' after Lacuna Vincta, the banded Chink Snail, for she will be my hard shell as long as I live in the sub tidal region, and because she is to me a gap in knowledge, an extended silence. I will step into her.

My mouth was watering with the language and the underwater otherworld. Kathryn called us over to introduce us to the manager of Taigh Chearsabhagh.

'Andy, this is Beady and this is Shuna.' We shook hands.

'So, are you Donald Shaw's sister then?' Shuna nodded in surprise. 'Anna-Wendy was in a couple of nights ago at the opening and told me that you were staying at hers. She told me about your trip.'

'Donald's sister?' asked Kathryn. 'I know him from my Glasgow days. I've got a very embarrassing story, will tell you later.' She was laughing.

'See, it really is a small world,' I said.

'The exhibition, it's beautiful, what a remarkable woman,' I said to Andy.

'You do realise it's all made up?' he said.

'What?' I felt like I'd been punched in the gut. I went and sat in the submersible, thinking about it. Well, why did it need to change anything, whether she was real or not? She is here, this is her story, over there is her swimming costume and on the wall are her words. What difference does it make whether she was real or not? But I was shaken. I listened to the underwater sounds, gullibility sticking in my gullet.

'So, it's a big fat lie,' Shuna said, joining me. 'It's so well done.'

I wanted to enjoy the artistry of it, but I've never been one for practical jokes. Those few seconds of another's discomfort have always been excruciating to me, when a laugh is had at someone else's expense. I was taking this personally, I realised.

We bought Kathryn a present in the shop, a jug glazed in all the blues of this island. On the way back to her house she told us the story of Donald and his harmonium.

'When I was a producer, one of the things I produced was a Gaelic Country Music series called 'Ceol Country' with Donald organising all the arrangements. He's great, it was so much fun working with him. We were filming every night for, I dunno, seven nights or whatever it was, down in Glasgow. One night we finished really late and I offered him a lift home in my car, which at that time was a banger of an old Golf. He had his harmonium with him and when we got to his house he couldn't open the boot. I got out and pressed the button and the whole thing fell onto the road. Oh my God, it was awful! He might have had insurance to get it reconditioned, but I just felt awful. I thought I am never ever giving anyone a lift with a really precious instrument again.'

'But it could have happened to anybody,' said Shuna.

'Do you know, he couldn't have been nicer about it, but I can still see all the gear falling out and it was too heavy to catch. I could also see he was upset, and quite rightly so.'

'Do you know what happened to him?' said Shuna. 'He had someone else's harmonium in his car, quite recently, I think, and his car was stolen. I think that's worse, he just felt so bad that he hadn't taken it out of the car, it was stolen overnight. It was an old old old old one, irreplaceable.'

'Harmoniums are iffy things to travel about with, it seems,' I said.

It had turned into a dry sunny afternoon but the wind was fierce. The flagpole outside Donnie and Peigi's house snapped in the north easterly. The ponies were grazing, bums to the wind, apparently oblivious to the sound. Donnie and Peigi had us in for a cup of tea and we gave them wine and chocolate, a token for their kindness in having the ponies for the night. They asked about the ponies, and our trip. Donnie told us about the tracks on the hill that he remembered from when he was a boy. 'They had three ruts', he said, 'two for the cart's wheels, one in the middle for the pony. You can still see those three tracks out on the hill today, the old peat tracks, they don't go anywhere though, just stop out on the hill. No use for getting through to someplace else. You're better sticking to the coast for that.'

We followed Kathryn and Akiko across the machair towards the Udal peninsula. The wind savaged the strips of plastic silage bale caught in the fences. It spooked the horses and snatched our words away. We rode across cultivated fields, past a wide shiny tractor and its trailing cloud of wind-spattered gulls. We topped the dunes and Tràigh Iar (meaning west beach) spanned out in front of us. It was one of those moments when your senses take off. I shouted something unintelligible at the top of my voice. The cold wind intensified the colours: Vallay was an emerald green banner unfurling on our left; straight ahead, way out across the citrine sand the sea was a strip of dark aquamarine. Our world was a bright whip of mane and tail and marram grasses, and our smiles spun off into the sand. Kathryn and Akiko led the way down the dunes towards where the line of white-finned waves met the shore.

'How about a gallop then?' shouted Kathryn when we caught up, and off we went. There was no way we could keep up with Akiko who raced ahead through the waves. The three-beat of the canter turned into the smooth four-beat of the gallop. Ross and Chief took it in turns to overtake each other and everything was wide open: no walls, gates, fences, bogs, people, just smooth wide beach. Exhilarated and laughing we left the beach at the far end. The ponies felt ten feet high, how rarely they get the chance to really move like that. And for them to let us taste the expansion and speed and freedom their DNA is built on. What a privilege.

Kathryn was taking us to a wheelhouse. Finally we'd actually see one, it seemed. We rode past a coil of rope up in the dunes, a black zigzag of pitch decorated its coils. It was like a giant adder, as big as a sleeping pony, asleep in the sun, tucked in out of the wind, basking.

Snakes. Mum had been obsessed with them. Snakes and Spiders and all 'creepy crawlies', as she called them. When Brèagha, her first grandchild, was born she'd refused to be known as Granny or Grandma. Instead she chose to be known as 'Lolo', from 'chongololo', a Giant African Millipede. So Lolo she was. That day after her death when my brothers and I were emptying the Luton van there had been a whole box of insect and reptile books. On the top was a hardback with REPTILES written simply on its cover in block capitals. Below was a high resolution photo of a Chameleon. Mum had loved her reptiles. She'd a touch of the Chameleon herself, could change in a flash, her mood, her allegiances, even her make-up. Stripes of Clinique and Dior in all the colours of Peacocks and Humming

Birds, strokes of iridescence that brought out the green in her eyes. Green like cats and witches.

Mum always said that witches were in the family. That her mother was a witch, that she'd killed her own father, Mum's grandfather, with a curse. That's what she told us. I thought about the exhibition that morning. The Lacuna, 'a genus of small inter-tidal mollusc: a gap or vacancy, a prolonged silence, a missing piece of text or information'. Now I wanted to ask her more about my grandmother being a witch. I wanted to ask her more about so many things. I'd had that small opening, when she was dying and I was in softest love with her, when I could have talked to her. But I didn't step into it. None of us did. We'd followed her lead and not talked about her death. Not even mentioned it. She'd known when Will and Tom and I were called in to see the consultant, the one in Oban with a bedside manner like a blunt shovel, but Mum hadn't asked what she'd said. She didn't mention her own death, not once. Not like all those years before, when she'd gone in for her first brain surgery when I was fifteen. She'd come upstairs to talk to Tom and me. 'If I die, children, I want you to know that I've had a good life. A full life. I've got you three. I have loved deeply. I have adventured.' This time, twenty-three years later, she was saying nothing. The tumour had done what tumours do, grown or moved or devoured something vital, and she could no longer talk. We're left with a whole host of lacunae that will never be filled. I can guess and imagine, but I will never truly know. My memories of her are a palimpsest like the sea-licked Lichens on the rocks at our feet, merely a thin breathing skin over the unfathomable story of the rock.

'There it is,' said Kathryn, interrupting my thoughts, pointing across to a fenced off area. We could see stonework through the mercurial sway of Marram Grass. We tied the ponies to the fence and stepped over the stile.

'I'll stay here and keep an eye on the horses,' said Kathryn.

It was like entering another world, down there inside the circular walls, out of the wind. The stones were silver, striated, strangely bare. Most had no Lichen, they'd been under the sand for centuries, maybe millennia. On some the Lichen was just starting to settle, a pearlescent bloom. There was a single upright stone, black and smooth, knee-height. I was pulled towards it. I put both hands on the top. It was warm from the sun. At its base was a beak, feathers, pieces of stitched skin clinging to a fragile skeleton. I squatted down to look more closely. The beak was long, a baby Curlew perhaps. I thought of Angus Dunn's poem, *Last Look*:

> *Not an ounce on her more*
> *than was needed to cover*
> *her bones*

> *Her mouth open in sleep,*
> *she looked like a fledgling –*
> *just as she should look, ready for where she's going.*

At the end Mum had been birdlike, her eyes shining brightly but her fine feathers gone. No lucent eyeshadow or lipstick, no jewellery, no beautiful clothes, just practical garments that were easy for the nurses to dress her in. Things she'd have hated. Her bodyweight evaporating with each breath but her heart continuing to beat strongly. She was a survivor. That part of her got more obvious as the rest of her faded. No food for months, it seemed, and on she went. I like to think she was getting ready for where she was going, letting go, lightening her load. She didn't need to be fierce any more. Or full of fight. Or be fabulous. Or glamorous. Her heart beat on and on and on, because that's just who she was. Courageous, full-hearted. *Better to have loved and lost than not to have loved at all.* I could hear her words now.

I picked some Marram stems and covered the tiny bird, but it had been perfect as it was, lying there in the sunshine. So I laid the grasses underneath instead, realising with dismay that I had no beads with me, I'd left them in the saddlebags that were now in the pickup on Berneray. There was a snail shell lying nearby, a bruise of heliotrope just visible through the sun-bleaching. I placed the shell next to the bird. A land-lacuna, holding space for missing information, being filled with birdsong and the scent of sand and sea. I picked a primrose and placed it next to the bird and shell. Primroses were everywhere on this bit where the sheep couldn't graze, this circle of protection that held history and bones and long-forgotten dreams in its sand-buried walls.

We got back on the ponies and cantered along the sandy paths. They were exalted and happy to run in their group of three. We trotted down onto the wide sands of *Tràigh Ear* (meaning east beach) on the other side of the Udal peninsula.

'That's where the well is that I told you about,' said Kathryn, pointing back towards the north of the peninsula. 'It's in amongst the rocks down by the shore. It can be tricky to find. The water's beautiful. I think I heard somewhere that it's where the summering cattle used to go to drink.' We still had twelve miles to ride to Berneray and it was already getting on for six o'clock. We agreed to save the well for another time and rode for a while further across sand now covered in a thin film of sea. The west beach of Berneray was visible as a chink of white in the north, the hills of Harris dozing in blues behind.

'Okay, I'd better be getting back, girls. It was lovely to ride with you. Come back again one day!'

The A865 was quiet, so were we. Every now and again we'd ride past a house and catch a scent of dinner cooking. We passed the loch and its dun where the Swan family had crossed earlier, and I imagined the family of eight now bobbing on the sea, the cygnets growing used to the salt, the swash of kelp. On the B893 to Berneray we got off the ponies. It was good to walk, watching our shadows striding long-legged across peaty pools and hill grass turning rose in the evening light. A Redshank pipped at us from a post, his legs skinny carmine. We turned right where the sign said, 'Sound of Harris Ferry'. We were getting nearer and the ponies sensed it. They stepped out lightly. It was nearly ten o'clock and the sun hovered on the horizon. It gilded everything to our left, the Cotton Grass, the grazing Sheep, the sea, in silver and platinum, while to our right the world was tinted with gold and rose-madder. We rode across to Berneray, loving that we had the causeway to ourselves. I lifted my face upwards, tasting all that pink light and wishing I wore feathers in my hair.

DAY FOURTEEN
Berneray to Harris

It was the 31st, the last day in May, the Celtic month of love. I was sitting at the big table in Berneray Hostel, not feeling the love at all. It was breakfast-time busy and I wanted solitude.

'I wasn't okay, you know, last night when you came in so late,' said the tight-lipped lady, looking me full in the eye. It must have been her who'd shone a head-torch in my face as I got into bed. Okay, so it had been after 11pm, but this was a hostel and we were being quiet as mice. Unlike the man in the bunk under her, perhaps her husband, the one she was now hassling about what to put in the lunch box, who had talked in his sleep. *Looking for joy*, he'd said distinctly at one point during the night.

'There's a lot to be said for Latin to be the lingua franca in Europe.' A man at the end of the table was holding court, talking over the others. This same man had just told me he was a musician. He had volunteered this randomly. I hadn't asked him who or what he 'was'. He seemed so self-satisfied, this was something Mum used to say about people and was as damning in her eyes as people being 'boring'.

It was evenings sitting around a big wooden table, not dissimilar to that one in the hostel, that I remember most about the Cairnholy years. It was where all the talking got done, and where almost everything got done. The rest of the house was too blisteringly cold. I'd recently seen Allan Wright, a family friend, and one of the very few people that would regularly visit Cairnholy. He'd been in Argyll on a work trip taking photographs and had come to stay. Allan, Martin and I had sat at our table, the same table he'd so often sat at thirty years earlier in Dumfries and Galloway, and shared memories. It was refreshing for me hearing him talk about Mum.

'She would decimate people with great artistry,' he laughed, 'but she was so lovable, as long as you were on the right side of the fence!' He'd talked about her 'nose for authenticity', how she 'didn't suffer fools gladly' and 'abhorred snobbishness'. That last made me smile. How did that fit, when I remember her talking about people being 'common'? But it did fit, of course it fitted, because she was that woman chock-full of contradictions. She hadn't belonged in any camp, box or social class. She was a free radical, roaming at will, cherry-picking from cultures and classes whatever appealed to her in any given moment. Wrinkling her nose at that which didn't. Retaining the right to change her mind on a whim, to scorn or revere, to love or hate, to support or drop like a stone.

'I'm just nipping out to the pickup. Do you want anything?' Shuna asked, interrupting my thoughts.

'Yes, my diary, please, I want to check the ferry times for tomorrow.'

After eating scrambled eggs we went into the sunshine with our coffee. Group photos were now taking place when earlier there'd been a flurried exchange of email addresses. Mr Lingua Franca was holding the camera. He shouted 'sex', everyone laughed and suddenly they were all gone, a mass exodus of good cheer and hi-vis.

'Bliss,' I said to Shuna as silence descended. I loved our shared company more and more with each passing day. Who else could I have made this trip with? Nobody else.

The coffee was lifting my mood. It was a glorious day. White cumulus clouds scudded high above the thatched roofs of the hostel buildings.

'Shit!' I said to Shuna, looking up from my diary. 'Our ferry is booked for today!'

'That can't be right. We're here for a day and a half.' I checked again. 'Today's the 31st, right? Our ferry is today, we've somehow lost a day.'

We talked about trying to change our tickets, but the ferries were so busy we knew that was unlikely. Also, we had rooms booked in Leverburgh for that night. We reconciled ourselves to making the most of the few hours we had left on Berneray. We had until 3pm to explore, but the loss of a day meant we only had a few hours to sort grazing in Leverburgh too. Ruari in Leverburgh had given us the name of a woman who might be able to help. We were waiting to hear back but sailing close to the wind.

'Let's check on the ponies and go and see Jinny,' said Shuna. 'She's been amazing.' It was Jinny who had given us the contacts of Naomi on Barra, Sue on Benbecula, and had sorted the ponies' grazing on Berneray where she lived.

'Wow, a field has just fallen from heaven!' said Shuna, looking at her phone. 'That's Kathryn in Leverburgh. She's got a field we can use for the ponies. I'll just text and say it's today not tomorrow we're coming, check if that's okay.'

We packed our stuff into the pickup and headed back to the ferry terminal where Chief and Ross had spent the night on Jinny's grazing. Common Seals were basking on the skerries along the rocky shoreline, their silver bellies on show. Meanwhile Shuna was looking on the other side of the road. 'They have such cool tractors over here.' The tractor in question was particularly glorious, being newly painted alizarin red, with a gleaming black funnel. Immaculate and loved.

As we arrived at Jinny's croft house on the Borve road a man in a green boiler suit was leaving. 'Hello, I'm Hector,' he said, extending a hand and a steady look from the most beautiful Prussian blue eyes, before walking purposefully towards a new agricultural building behind the cottage. Everything looked very well cared for.

'You'll have to excuse me, moving so slowly,' said Jinny, welcoming us into her home. She nodded down at her leg in plaster. 'I broke it checking the cows on the hill.' She said it very matter-of-factly. That was her. Astonishingly matter-of-fact and equally industrious, we quickly learnt. As well as her full-time job for Anderson Banks legal firm, 'my patch is Berneray down to Vatersay', she also had a catering business. Warm jars of strawberry jam were stacked on the sideboard. We chatted ponies, she had an Eriskay called Lilly, and the original plan had been that she'd ride with us today.

'I can't believe you won't be going to the West Beach with the ponies. The riding here is just stunning,' she said.

'Another time,' we assured her. 'We'll just have to come back.' I think Shuna and I were feeling equally embarrassed by our haphazard timetabling, highlighted by Jinny's extreme efficiency. There was her knitting business too. She brought a traditional Eriskay gansey through for us to look at.

'I've just finished this. Every single one I make is unique,' she said, 'and there is a waiting list for orders.' The jumper was cream-coloured, and a brown label said: 'Handmade on the Isle of Berneray. jinny@hebrides.net.'

'That is beautiful,' I said, stroking the complicated pattern. 'How on earth do you have time for this?'

'I like to be busy,' she said. 'I went down to Eriskay to learn from two ladies down there. There are only a few people left with the knowledge of the old patterns, so I feel very fortunate to have learned the skill. I run classes up here from time to time. We don't want these skills to die out.' She and Hector had moved back to his family's croft when he retired from the RAF. 'I've never looked back,' she said. 'Love it here.'

We asked her what she'd do if she were us, with just a few hours to explore. 'I'd go up there,' she said, without hesitating, pointing at the small hill visible through her kitchen window. 'There's so much up there. Try not to break a leg though.' She laughed. 'There's a cairn at the top, every time Hector's grandfather walked there he'd take a stone to add to it. Boats used the cairn to guide them in. The hill is called Being a'Chlaidh, (Hill of the Graveyard) and there is a standing stone eight feet in height and what used to be a chapel, what's left of it anyway, and a chair stone. Local folks stole the stones from the chapel for lintels when they were building their houses, some say it has brought bad luck, there are a lot of widows on the Borve road.'

'I'd like to see Angus MacAskill's birthplace too,' said Shuna.

'Oh yes, Angus the giant, you'll need to visit his old house. There's a Viking Court too, down on the machair, and there's a chair stone there as well where the accused is supposed to have sat. They say they used to chop people's heads off on the chair then bury them at Cnoc nan Claigeann, (Hillock of the Heads). There's also a Viking pier. Oh, and the faerie milk holes down by the shore too of course.'

My ears pricked up. 'Faerie milk holes, what are they?'

'Small round holes in the rocks. The locals used to fill them with milk to appease the faeries, so the story goes.'

'Can you show me on the map where they are?'

'See here, you can actually drive all the way to Angus MacAskill's monument. If you walk from there, the faerie milk holes are somewhere along this bit, see where the shore gets rockier. You might have trouble finding them though.'

We said our goodbyes, promising to be back one day to ride on West Beach with her, and wishing her a speedy recovery with her leg.

'Angus MacAskill, 1825 to 1863,' Shuna said, reading from a plaque that was mottled gold with Old Man's Beard. 'Within these walls Aonghas Mór MacAskill was born. Known as the Nova Scotia Giant he was the son of Norman MacAskill who emigrated in 1831. Standing seven feet nine inches in height and without pathological defect, he achieved many feats of strength and is remembered as a kindly and just man and a humble Christian.' Nearby was a cairn built to his exact height, Shuna stood beside it, completely dwarfed. 'My friend Jock,' Shuna said, 'once told me about the MacAskills that came from Dunvegan on Skye, they were big men, and one of them was over seven feet tall. I wonder if they're related.'

We walked across the machair towards Loch Borve Bay, also known as Cockle Beach. The plan was to cross the sand to the opposite shore and look for the faerie milk holes, then head up the hill to the cairn, keeping an eye out along the way for the other sites Jinny had mentioned. Empty cockles were scattered everywhere, some were being blown across the sand leaving little wavy tracks behind them.

On the other side of the bay my eye was drawn to some smooth black slabs of rock, no faerie milk holes though. We continued checking out the surfaces of the rocks, and then there they were, about a foot apart, two perfectly symmetrical sea-spun holes. They were about the circumference of an egg cup at the bottom, getting wider towards the outer edge. *Oh, thank you, Jinny.* I took out the bead purse and, thinking of Mum's grandchildren, picked out a selection of Swarovski crystals. Their tiny facets coruscated in the sunlight as I dropped them into the nearest hole.

'That's a lot of beads,' said Shuna enquiringly.

'For her grandchildren,' I said. 'Seven of them. She never met the four youngest, they were all born after she died.'

'That must be hard for your brothers,' she said. I picked up

172

the bead purse again. *Now, which one for Mum?* A jade bead caught my eye. I placed it in the second fairy hole, it looked exquisite against the sea-darkened rock. Jade, a stone that was favoured in ancient times for its durability, its ability to sharpen made it a favourite for axe heads and knives.

We daundered up the hill, discovering one treasure after another: the ruined chapel – lintels missing, rocks laced with pink quartz, the single standing stone, huge and yearning towards the island of Boreray to our west. Grassy tumps starred with shards of iron-blue mussel shell. Marsh Orchids and purple Field Gentians. The warm air smelt of sea and turf and tiny flowers, the Meadow Pippets' high piping was everywhere as we climbed. I had to agree with the Scottish writer Jessie Kesson: *May is poignant, the birdsong is at its sweetest now. Nothing touches the human being more than smell and song. May is the month of both.* By the time we found the chair stone we were both hungry and took turns sitting on it while we ate our lunch.

'Hard to imagine anything gruesome happening here,' I said, as Shuna finished a can of sardines. After lunch I leant back on the stone chair and caught up with my note taking; reading the notes months later I was taken back to that windblown day: *Sound of corncrakes coming up from below/A big bee just flew by – very fast/Singing skylights.* I guessed I'd meant 'skylarks' not 'skylights'.

After lunch we made our way to the cairn now visible on top of the hill. We carried our own stones to add to it. From the cairn we could make out Ross and Chief down in the south-east corner of the island, and the sweep of ultramarine sea between Berneray and North Uist, rounded into two by the arc of the causeway. 'We'd better head back,' said Shuna, as if reading my thoughts of missing the ferry.

We walked quickly back down the hill, watching where we placed our feet, feeling the wind on our backs and the sun on our faces. A stone caught my eye, it seemed to be flickering. Fibres of wool were quivering in the wind, trapped by the Velcro grip of Lichen. The Lichen was a deep tourmaline. I thought of the woven pictures that had been on the walls of my grand-parents' house in Anglesey, pieces Mum had made while still at school. Six-foot-long vermiculate designs made of wool and all in autumn colours. That same tourmaline green, and umber and rust and mustard yellows, crafted with consummate skill. I wondered now what stories those welts of wool were telling. Had she already met Dad, fallen in love? Growing up, in that fraught space between Mum and Dad, it had been hard for me to imagine that they'd ever been in love.

'We are so completely jammy,' Shuna said, flinging her arms out wide.

A second later I adjusted my foot mid-stride above two Oystercatcher eggs. The shells were sienna – a shade darker than the blonde hill grass they lay on – and splattered in inky squiggles. 'Shuna, come and see this!' We looked at the eggs in delight and, without thinking, I bent down and touched one. It was warm. 'Quick, we'd better get out of here.' We hurried down towards the shore, Oystercatcher alarm calls zigzagging behind us.

At the faerie milk holes I unzipped the purse. I needed to leave a bead here for Dad too. Lapis lazuli, a stone that histori-cally was used to make ultramarine pigment, which I rolled in beside Mum's bead. Perfect. Double perfect.

'How's your trip going so far? I heard they nearly didn't let you on the Eriskay crossing.' The ticket collector on the MV Loch Portain crinkled his eyes against the sun. 'What are you doing once you get to Leverburgh?'

'Someone called Kathryn has a field at Strond that the ponies can use,' Shuna answered, handing our tickets through the window.

'I know exactly where you are. Not far for you to go at all.'

We sat up on deck during the sixty-minute sailing. As the ferry changed course between clusters of islets we moved to keep out of the wind. Binoculars, and seabirds, were out in force, and for the first time I had lens envy. Maybe I should look into buying a really good pair of small binoculars. Once again, I wished I was better able to distinguish between all these magnificent diving gliding seabirds. One woman said to another, 'There is no such thing as a gull.' Once in a while we stood and looked down on the vehicle deck. All seemed quiet. An indigo camper van was parked close behind the horsebox, *Living the Dream* emblazoned in white cursive letters above the windscreen. Watching the low sand-lipped islands of Berneray and North Uist slipping away, I was already missing the beaches and the machair. Our planning for the next bit of the trip was virtually non-existent, and the rock-scarred hills of Harris looked dark and foreboding beyond the ferry's bow. *What if the best of the trip is already past?*

We followed Kathryn's car along the single-track road to Strond where the croft was. Her two youngest children, still in their navy primary school uniforms, had ear-to-ear grins when we introduced them to Ross and Chief, before racing off to prepare milk for the three pet lambs. Gruffalo, Sparky and Floppy would be the ponies' companions for the next couple of nights.

'Will that be okay for them?' asked Kathryn. 'The field?'

'It's perfect,' we answered. Kathryn explained that the lambs were from Pabbay. She pointed to an island in the far distance where her husband was farm manager, and where he spent weeks at a time completely alone.

'It's a beautiful place,' she said. 'We go over when we can, but there are no ferries.' A car stopped beside us on the road, and two teenage girls started talking in Gaelic. Kathryn turned and introduced them to us in English, friends of her eldest daughter who was away. 'She'll be mad to miss you, she has a Highland pony herself.' The girls drove off and we chatted while the lambs vigorously drained their bottles. Kathryn recommended dinner at the Anchorage Restaurant. 'It's fabulous but you'll need to phone ahead for a table. It's very popular these days.' By the time we headed back to Leverburgh, and the Bunkhouse, the sky had clouded over and the sea was darkening to deep slate.

The Anchorage was a busy place and everything was delicious, oysters and hand-dived scallops and the tastiest monkfish either of us had ever eaten. We finished off with a malt whisky: *Poit Dubh 8yr (Island). A blended malt from Skye, peaty, earthynose, spicy with maritime salinity on the palate; a finish of depth with some heat.* We recognised the two young Irish men from our room at the hostel, heads close, hands on glasses of wine, deep in conversation and love. We were sharing our room with a fifth person, a heavy-voiced woman from Fife. She'd also eaten at the Anchorage, and later, back at the hostel as the Irish couple and ourselves were raving about our meals, she told us that she'd 'made the wrong choice.' I sensed that may have been a habit of hers. Her bed in the hostel was also a wrong choice, and her length of stay, and the weather too. My heart went out to her, for all her moaning she was hardy. She'd always wanted to travel the Hebrides, she said, and now that her husband was dead she was fulfilling her dream.

'If you eat at the Anchorage again try the scallops,' I suggested, thinking she could do with a few radial blessings. *And a nice dram might help too.*

DAY FIFTEEN
Getting Organised

A man hoovered around us with high energy as we sat under an upturned boat hanging from the ceiling in the hostel's common room. Our maps were laid out in front of us. Shuna and I had taken our time to get up, chatting from our bunk beds while we waited for the noise in the kitchen to subside. We weren't in any hurry, having already decided to take today to get sorted with our route through Harris. To date we had the offer of a field for the ponies in Horgabost and a bed for us in Tarbert. After the safe and sandy feel of the southern Hebrides we had a growing sense of the inaccessibility of Harris and Lewis: the expansive bogs, high hills, shortage of good paths and fast busy roads. Anna-Wendy back at Baileshare had told us that Ruari, the owner of Am Bothan, had walked every inch of Harris and would be a great man to talk to. He'd promised to look at the maps with us that morning.

'Should we move?' we asked the hooverer, as he whipped the red Henry past us.

'Nah, you're fine,' he said. 'I'm nearly done.'

'That's how we get rid of people,' Ruari said. 'Sometimes Bennie just gets the hoover out for the hell of it, you know, to move people on if they're getting a bit too comfortable.' I didn't think he was meaning us, but he might have been. Ruari was sharp, funny, attractive. He moved quickly, like a Peregrine. I felt dull-witted in his flickering gaze.

'What's this trip all about then?'

'We've always wanted to ride up the Hebrides,' I said tentatively.

'We've got a Facebook page, 21 *Pony Days in the Outer Hebrides*, if you want to have a look,' added Shuna.

'You're not fundraising, are you?'

I felt myself blushing. We were, and the Facebook page was to let people who had sponsored us follow our progress. We'd decided not to bring that up as we went along, people out here were already doing enough to help us. Asking for money has never been a forte of mine, and Ruari had hit a nerve.

'It's a low-key bit of fundraising for Friends of Plockton Music School,' I said. 'My daughter's there. It's a magic place, for kids with a passion in traditional music.' I kept talking, nervously. 'It's government funded, but it's experiencing severe cutbacks, and this seemed like a good opportunity.'

'I'm glad you haven't asked for a free room. I get a lot of people who think that because they're walking backwards with a wheelbarrow on their heads for charity they should get a free room.' He smiled and his words rang in the sudden silence as somewhere, out of sight, the hoover was turned off.

'So,' said Shuna, 'Anna-Wendy said you've done a lot of walking on Harris. Can we show you where we thought we'd ride? We're a bit flummoxed, to be honest, Barra and the Uists have been so easy, all that machair, must be some of the best riding in the world. Harris looks more limited, we might even have to stick to the roads.'

'Well, you could,' said Ruari, looking at where we'd drawn a possible route, mostly along roads, on the map, 'but that would be dull.'

We agreed and with Ruari's help came up with a new plan for the next four days. Shuna's face was flushed with excitement and I could feel my own was the same. Three days from now, all being well, we'd be right in the heart of Harris, at a place only accessible by boat, or foot, and hopefully by pony, although Ruari was giving no assurances not being a pony-man himself.

'If it's too hard we can just turn back,' Shuna and I agreed. We were both up for taking a chance.

Bennie, the energetic hooverer, had just appeared back, jeans and T-shirt gone and now dressed head-to-toe in red and black Paramo gear. He was wearing barefoot running shoes, no socks and was chewing gum furiously.

'These two are thinking of going into Kinloch Rèasort with their ponies. They should be able to pick a way through, shouldn't they?' Benny nodded. 'You know the beehive dwellings,' Ruari continued, pointing at the map, 'whereabouts would you say they were?' I'd been thrilled when he mentioned the beehive huts earlier. I'd wanted to see some ever since reading Alastair McIntosh's descriptions of these ancient dwellings in *Poacher's Pilgrimage*.

Bennie was pointing to a different spot on the map from Ruari. To be safe I circled both.

'Okay, that's me off,' Bennie said.

'Where's he going?' we asked, watching through the window as he hoisted his pack onto his back.

'Who knows?' he said. 'Could be anywhere, he's hardcore.'

Bennie was now facing away from us, his pack hiding his head, two paddles protruding from a side panel.

'He's got an inflatable paddle raft with him this time,' Ruari said. 'He'll be off to some uninhabited island. He's an adrenalin junkie.' I felt nerves tighten across my stomach. Bennie was everything we weren't. Prepared for any eventuality, every strap on his pack would be tensioned just right. He was the picture of taut travelling prowess: capable and able and absolutely on the case.

It was early afternoon by the time we finished packing, emailing and phoning, looking at the maps. We decided to take the pickup north and leave it near Tarbert where we'd be in two days' time. As we'd be riding up the west coast we decided to drive up the east side of Harris, on what they call 'The Golden Road', and stop at Rodel Church on the way. Rodel, like the beehive dwellings, had been brought to life for me in *Poacher's Pilgrimage*. I'd bought a pile of books to read before this trip, but this was the only one I'd finished, and the only one I'd brought on the trip. Earlier that day we'd both read the chapter about 'Saint Clement's Church of Rodel': *Of all the island's three dozen or so pre-Reformation chapels, only two have been restored, this is one of them (…) The church sits beneath the cloud-fringed summit of an iconic mountain, Roineabhal. It sits with its square lookout tower, tight-pressed into a rocky knoll with views down to the southern Hebrides. This, to my eye, in its setting on a rise above the sea, is quite the most exquisite little gem this side of Tuscany.*

We parked beside a deserted farmhouse and walked down to the church. The fields on either side were dotted with silver stones and white sheep and the grass was very green, evidence of the seam of limestone running through Rodel Glen. It was overcast but the light coming through the clouds was intense. The glossy leaves of the Flag Irises glinted bright as blades. Two vintage cars drove away from the church as we approached, wending their way northwards on The Golden Road. '*Toad of Toad Hall cars,*' Shuna said.

The place was other-worldly. We fell silent as we stepped amongst gravestones that spanned the centuries. There were the small unmarked stones that Alastair McIntosh calls 'plainsong' stones, and ancient hand-carved gravestones, the letters mere suggestions through aeons of lichen growth. There were newer stones too, black letters on white marble: *In loving Memory of John MacDonald/DROWNED THROUGH THE ICE/24TH JANUARY 1917/AGED 11 YEARS.*

I moved towards the warm tones of a cast-iron tombstone, elaborate and crumbling, and then stopped by a shiny granite stone, its surface smooth and un-favoured by lichen, erected for *Angus MacLeod who died at Quidinish, 20th March 1915* by his *sorrowing widow*. 'Sorrowing'. How much rounder and fuller it was than the word 'grieving'. I was drawn back, again and again, to the tiny leaning plainsong stones. One had a perfect hole through it. A bead-stone.

I joined Shuna and we followed the curved path up to the church. Oak doors opened into an interior of archways within archways, of bands of light falling through leaded windows onto sole-shone flagstones. We were the only living people in that place.

'I love it here,' I said. So often I feel a sense of foreboding in churches, at times even terror, but I felt none of that in Rodel Church. We stood side by side in front of the stone-carved effigy of the '8th Chief of the Macleods'. He was being watched over by Angels and Dogs, strong-legged Deer and a birlinn in full sail. Shuna led the way up the steep stairway to the top of the tower. I was glad I wasn't alone as I felt the air press against my back, the hairs on my nape stand up. It was just a moment, and then the feeling was gone. We stepped across the wooden floor towards a tall slim window.

Silvered light fell over a pile of objects on the stone sill, hundreds of tiny gifts: a clove of garlic; twenty-pence pieces; a card which said *Our Lady of Mt Carmel – pray for us*; a bookmark with Italian words written across a snowy mountain scape; a garish pink plastic flower; a white shoelace; and shells, lots and lots of shells – mussels and limpits and cockles. There was also a silver charm bracelet, sweeties in wrappers, sheep's wool fresh from the field or fence. I put my hand into my pocket, feeling for what I knew was there. Not beads, but two tiny yellow winkle shells from Vallay. Blowing off the grains of sand I placed them on top of a polished two-pence piece.

Remembering the little model of the Virgin Mary that had been on Mum's bedside table while she was dying, I wondered what had happened to it. We wouldn't have thrown it away, but it was all such a blur. The days after her death, emptying her room in the nursing home. My brothers and I couldn't wait to get away from the smell of end-of-life that hit you when you were beeped in through the doors, the smell of urine and decline. We went down the tower's stairway, feeling with our feet in the darkness, one stone step at a time, until we were back in the earthy smell of old stone, and then outside, breathing in the sea.

'Let's look for the naked lady,' I said. Alastair McIntosh describes the 'Sheila-na-Gig' of Rodel as 'an astonishing stone-crafted figure' crouching on the south face of the church '*as if she's giving birth. Her womanhood is unconcealed in all its fullness. She nurses in her arms a heavily eroded figure that looks more like an animal, a lamb or seal, than the babe one might expect*'.

We walked around the church, looking upwards, eyes drawn to every detail; copper nails leaching verdigris into leadwork, the crenellated tower, the pink tones of the roofing slate. 'Look at him,' said Shuna, pointing upwards. A carving of a man wearing a shirt, but naked below, who appeared to be holding his penis in his two hands, above his perfectly round testicles.

'Well, he wasn't on the information board inside,' I said. We read later that he is known as 'Seumus a' Bhuid – James the

Willy', or 'The Lewd Man'. Further along we found the Sheila-na-Gig. She was high up and eroded by the weather, but there she was, nakedly squatting. Mum must have loved these two. I felt sure she would have come here on one of her trips.

Anything to do with willies would have her giggling, her canines on show, eyes sparkling. I'd catch her looking at men's crotches and later she'd pass comment. It wasn't just willies she was fascinated by. It was bodies and nakedness in general. When I was at secondary school, I used to have baths with my best friend and she would sometimes come into the bathroom, 'needing something from the cupboard'. *No, Mum, that's not okay*, I'd scream inside. But I didn't know how to deal with it. She and Paul fed off each other. They'd comment on my friend's body, and on other peoples' bodies. This provoked a prudishness in me. I'd rebel with my silent disapproval. They'd tell me not to be so 'po-faced' and laugh. They laughed a lot together. The more they laughed the more humourless I'd become, and the more I'd get it for being 'a misery'.

I looked up at Sheila-na-Gig, happy, naked, weather-worn. My hands had gone into hard fists at my sides. I unfurled them, smiled tentatively up at that lovely naked figure. 'We better get going,' said Shuna. I nodded and we walked away, leaving Seumus-the-Willy and Sheila-na-Gig to their sea and stargazing, to their slow erosion.

On the way out we passed a dead Rabbit, and another, an adult this time, and two more dead babies. It wasn't myxomatosis, their eyes were perfect. I bent to turn one over, no bullet wounds either. They were just lying there on the cut grass between the gravestones. 'That's so weird,' I said to Shuna, 'do you think they've been poisoned?'

I wished I hadn't seen them, those silken dead Rabbits. I tried to shake off the strange feeling as we walked back towards the pickup. I opened the glove compartment and took out a dark chocolate mint Kit Kat, broke it in two and handed half to Shuna. 'Let's go and see what this Golden Road is all about then,' she said, as the windscreen wipers cleared away rain that had just started to spit.

'It's more Heron Road than Golden Road,' I said, half an hour later. They were everywhere on that grey afternoon, standing alongside slate-still pools, watching, timelessly. We drove up and down, round sharp bends, through a landscape of water and stone and sheet-metal sky. There were Sheep too, their lambs small. You wondered how they survived, grazing goodness from between the rocks. And you wondered about the people in the past, who, like the Herons, had sought a bellyful from the water, and who, like the Sheep, had made the most of the thin soil. They would have had to be as watchful and patient as the Herons, as enduring as these Sheep with their slow-burning amber eyes. There were glimpses of opulence in that landscape too: the sleekit Seals draped over the skerries, the daubs of turquoise and rose keel on the Ewes' shoulders.

Houses dotted the landscape: ruins with rusting tin roofs and rotting window frames; up-kept houses with whitewashed walls; brand-new ones with flashing glass fronts. We drove past signs to Lingerbay, Manish Town, Geocrab, and all the time the road twisted and turned through endless eddies of rock.

'Do you know why it's called The Golden Road?' I asked.

'I think because the locals had to fight so hard to get the money from the authorities to build it.'

'Imagine what it was like before the road was built,' I said. 'I suppose most settlements were reached from the sea.'

We passed a steel-clad Nissan hut with *BOAT BUILDER J. MacAulay* in careful lettering above the rounded doors. I wondered if it was still in use. From the outside you'd think not, but inside, who knew what was hidden away from prying eyes and wrecking weather.

We could now see the A859, the main road that linked Tarbert with Leverburgh down the West coast, cutting across the hillside ahead of us. We decided to park at a Hydro Electric station where there was plenty of turning room, and where hopefully the trailer wouldn't be in anyone's way. We locked the doors and set off down the main road heading back to Leverburgh, both of us putting out our thumbs when we heard a car coming. The first car that passed didn't slow down for us, nor the next, nor the next. This continued for an hour and a half. There was very little traffic. It was well after seven o'clock now, but still I couldn't believe that no one was stopping for two women, cleaner than we'd been for days and not at all scary-looking. My thoughts turned dark as I walked along the bright white line, loose chippings flying up every time a car sped past. Umber peat cuttings opened on each side of the road. I could feel tears surfacing with each hard tarmac footfall. I felt vulnerable, and ashamed, and was too embarrassed to share my feelings with Shuna.

Finally, a little white car stopped and a man jumped out. Moving bags and books off the back seat he said, 'I'm only going as far as Horgabost.' We were delighted to get a lift however far, having realised by then that we might be walking all the way to Leverburgh. Peter asked us questions and was enthusiastic about our trip. He'd moved up from London a few years earlier, was a writer and journalist and on his way back from the swimming pool in Tarbert. When we told him we'd be camping at Horgabost the following night he invited us round for dinner. 'See you tomorrow night then,' we said cheerily as we got out.

Peter had changed our luck. Within minutes a woman from Leverburgh picked us up. She was chatty and friendly, and told us how she and her husband had moved up years before, leaving behind a rock-music scene and a very different life in England. She dropped us outside the bunkhouse.

We were hungry and ready for a drink. I felt subdued by how I'd faltered, how low I'd got walking along that road, but we were back now amongst friendly faces. A couple were talking about St Kilda, where they were heading next day, her sixtieth birthday present. Her excitement was infectious. There were spaces on the boat, why didn't we go, it was the chance of a lifetime. We thought about it but decided to stay on course. St Kilda would remain the sudden thrill of that night on Vallay when we'd seen a cone of mauve crown the horizon. I started chopping onions, and by the time Shuna handed me a glass of extra dry Prosecco tears were pouring down my face.

DAY SIXTEEN

Leverburgh to Horgabost

Ross and Chief watched us from where they were tied up at the wall. Tarpaulins, weighted down over the tidy peat stack between us, fussed in the wind. We set off towards Leverburgh, all of us glad to be on the move once again. Blackface ewes called throatily to their lambs as we passed. They watched, jaws stilled just long enough to make sure we weren't a threat, before resuming their clockwise chewing. A plaque set off from the road said *Site from which Harris Tweed was first marketed by the Paisley Sisters*. The lettering below was eroded, I could only make out the word *home* and the date *1864*. A fine rain had been falling all morning, but now there was a bite of blue overhead and everything glistened. It was the first time we'd seen full sun on Harris. Between the smattering of small islands mud flats were inscribed with silver water runnels, and Shelducks guddled, flashes of white and chestnut.

As we arrived back at Leverburgh an ovation of purple irises halted us in our stride. We waited as a capped man passed by with his dog, two ewes and a lamb. Behind them a rainbow lifted over the tumbledown tin cottage on Ferry Road. We passed the Church of Scotland on our right, the Community Shop on our left, before stopping in front of the primary school where Kathryn worked. She'd asked us if we'd call in on our way past so the children could meet the ponies. The children came out in waves of high spirits and red sweatshirts. First the nursery children, then the Gaelic class, then the class that is taught in English. How fabulous to have the choice like that. Chief was delighted to meet the chattering children, extending his muzzle for rubs, but Ross didn't feel quite right to me, shifting his weight from one foot to another.

'I'm a bit worried about Ross,' I said as we left. 'He seems odd.' We rode into the car park at the Church of Scotland and I hopped off. As I went to check his feet, he straddled his hind legs, and with a great sigh began to pee. The pee went on, and on, and on. In the midst of this seemingly never-ending stream the church door opened and the minister stepped out, his white collar flashing as he hurried to his car, his long coat wrapped around him against the wind. I lifted my hand in a giggle-ridden greeting. I think he nodded in our direction, but couldn't be sure. And still the pee was coming, a veritable river was now running down the tarmac slope of the car park. The car reversed speedily then drove past, through the pee-torrent, and out onto the road. Finally, with another great sigh Ross brought his back legs back up underneath himself.

'The timing! Oh my God,' I said, looking up at Shuna. 'I have never seen such a huge pee, it went on forever. I hope the minister didn't take offence.'

'Ross must have been desperate,' Shuna said. 'They hate peeing on concrete because of the splashes.'

'Oh, Ross,' I said, turning to him, 'I bet you feel better now.' Still laughing we unpacked our waterproofs. The sky had turned dark and it looked like heavy rain was on its way. Just retribution perhaps.

We turned off the main road and headed north towards Loch na Moracha, and the point on the map where we'd drawn in pencil the route of the Hebridean Way. This was a new walking route from Vatersay to the Butt of Lewis. It wasn't on our OS map but was a stretch of new pathway that would enable us to miss out a few miles of main road. The sun was shining again. Snipe snipped across the moor on either side of us and the wind whisked away our words. We left the road where a brand-new sign said *Hebridean Way, Sgarasta/Scarista 7km/4.4m*. The path cut across the low-lying land north of the loch to skirt the slopes of Ben Mùla, a small rounded hill 271 metres at the summit. From somewhere on its treeless slopes a Cuckoo was calling. We set off down the path which was made of some kind of membrane laid over the peat, and skimmed with a layer of gritty surface. I felt the magic of following a new path.

'It's amazing how much the ground is moving under Ross's hooves,' said Shuna from behind. 'The ponies don't seem to mind though.'

The path meandered through stacks of peats, freshly cut and drying in the sun between shoals of Bog Cotton. Ahead was a brand-new, stainless steel foot-gate, easily wide enough for ponies where the path changed. Two ditches ran alongside a raised pathway. It looked like a machine had dug trenches and put the peat on top of the central strip. Leaving the ponies to graze we went for a look. We stepped on the foot-worn path down the middle, even without the ponies the whole thing wobbled softly. We walked on wondering if it would hold the ponies' weight, some hopeful part of us believing that surely it had been made sound enough to take the weight of ponies.

'It's not very far before the path hits the harder hill,' I said optimistically.

'Yes, it's not far,' said Shuna. 'Maybe we could take the saddles and gear off and carry that across ourselves.' I looked down, imagining what would happen if the ponies stepped into the ditches, or jumped across to the peat bog beyond. Up close the water in the ditches was black as oil. I came to my senses with a jolt.

'Shuna, if we're worried enough to take the saddles off, why are we even considering it? There's no need to take a risk here, we can get to Scarista along the road.'

'Yup, let's go back to the ponies, make a coffee and head back along the road.'

Ross was standing still, snoozing, I thought, but when I got closer I saw that the whole saddle and all the bags had slipped round and was hanging almost under his belly. He stood with his body patiently rebalancing, with a look of such forbearance in his eyes that I blushed.

'You are a star, Ross,' I said, undoing the girth and with Shuna's help lifting the saddle and packs back on. I physically didn't have the strength on my own.

'Why did they put the path right across the middle of a bog?' I asked. 'There must be so much local knowledge about path building. Why not ask people who know about these things? Look, the path could have circled round the low hill, avoiding the bog.' Shuna took the stove out of its mesh bag, and placed each spidery leg with care. During the whole trip I didn't set up the stove once.

'Seems such a shame,' she said, 'to go to all this expense and not build a path to last. Some of the paths we've ridden the past few years, hundreds of years old and still in good condition. I hope the art isn't being lost.'

Buzzing with coffee we led the ponies back towards the road. The bronze in Ross's coat glinted as sunshine spilt between clouds. A car was parked near the sign and two people were working at the peats. In their seventies, or maybe their eighties, the lady was working in a skirt. They didn't raise their heads as we passed, not even when we said hello, but the woman's hands paused in their stacking and I caught her eye for a fleeting second. She had the same look of forbearance and stalwartness as Ross. I felt insubstantial, unworthy, foolish. It was good to step back onto the tarmac road.

'That was a close one,' I said, as we both looked back at the quaking path, its glinting silver ditches. It was sobering to think we'd even momentarily entertained the thought of carrying on along that path. A strange mist can come down on a long ride which can make carrying on feel like a very good idea, when clearly it isn't. We'd have to watch out for that mist. Then the morning's weather met us head on. We tucked our chins, squinted our eyes, and trotted forwards into the wind and rain feeling chastened and chilled.

Our waterproofs were dry again by the time we stepped onto the sand before Sgarasta on the West coast. Ross took long strides, happy to feel the soft give of sand after the plod of the road miles. We rode past salt marshes being grazed by sheep and red cattle. To the west, across amber-flecked tidal shallows, was the smooth bulge of Gob an Tobha, toe head. The lower slopes were bright green, above was a heather-brown crown run through with an arc of quartz. The clouds had bunched into blooms of white and the smell of the sea was getting stronger. Ross and Chief strode along side by side, manes spun to ringlets by the wind. We rode up onto a bank of dunes, a new sound reached us, waves, as they unravelled against the moon crescent of Sgarasta beach that swept three golden miles to the north east.

'The colours!' I gasped. The sun swept a spotlight of aquamarine across water that pulsed with bands of turquoise and teal. The horizon was a deep Prussian blue holding up the hills of North Harris. It was hard to take it all in, the gold of the sand where the sun lit it, the startlingly white seahorses surging in, the unfathomable sweep of colours through the sea. We stood and stared as our feet sank into the deep dry sand, and the Marram spun against our legs.

Shuna sat down and Chief and Ross stood behind her, drifting into snooze mode, while I walked down the steeply sloping beach to the water's edge. The waves were somersaults of sapphire breaking on the beach, leaving finely drawn lines on the sand. Then followed the sucking backwash, a storm of sand and white bubbles. I crouched down and watched as each new wave re-drew the line in the sand between wet and dry, foam-topped peaks coming a little higher all the time. I chose my bead, there was no question. I held it in my hand, a flame-lamped glass bead, which, like the sea in front of me, almost defied definition: colours within colours within colours, seams of blue-greens and green-blues. *I wonder where you got this one from, Mum, it's exquisite.*

I placed the bead a couple of feet above the bubbling tideline. Tiny Clams came into focus, smooth shells decorated with concentric circles of gradated colour: this one, all pinks; this one, almost pearlescent whites; that one, dove greys. There were tiny broken mussel shells too, fragments of electric and cobalt blue. As the sea sucked back with each wave my insides turned over. I watched the sun chase tracks of turquoise full-tilt across the sea and wanted to follow out west to Tir nan Og, to the place that Seton Gordon describes as the *land set beneath the horizon of the Atlantic (…) where one may meet, in perpetual youth and in all the glory of their strength and beauty, many of those who are counted great and worthy of memory.* I placed the bead gently and stood up. I didn't want to be there in the moment that the sea took it away, I wanted to remember this bead on the cusp between worlds. I walked up the beach towards Shuna and the ponies, not looking back, hearing the boom of the surf and a Cow calling faraway.

The ponies had woken up and were grazing on the Marram with a rhythmical soft tearing sound that made my mouth water. We ate smoked mussels, oatcakes speckled with sunflower seeds, dark chocolate. Shuna had the map out. 'I think that's where we're going, we'll be passing through those hills the day after tomorrow.' The hills of North Harris were dark. I wished they were in sunshine, I think that would have reassured me. 'See that steep-sided clip on the skyline, that's Sròn Scourst, I think, and the track out to Kinloch Rèasort will pass below that.'

Shuna lay back on the sand. I got out my notebook and turned to the back. *Mum's Playlist*, I wrote at the top of the page. Where to start? The Highland pipes, she'd loved them, *they give me goosebumps*, she used to say, pure delight spreading across her face every time we heard them:

1. Pibroch (which one?)
2. 'American Pie' – Don MacLean

The memories flooded in. Mum singing along, sunshine streaming through a window, her hair long and red. She was ironing, it must have been in Wales, I never remembered her ironing after Wales.

3. 'Perfect Day/Walk on the Wild Side' – Lou Reed

Mum singing aloud again, *and the coloured girls go doo do doo do too do do doo*, freewheeling in the vintage Rover 90 down a hill on Anglesey, the three of us shouting *faster, faster*, her telling us not to lean against the doors in case they opened, the smell of old leather and wood.

4. 'Escape is so Simple' – Cowboy Junkies

I could picture the cassette tape – *The Caution Horses* – sitting on the table in her workshop at Cairnholy, the gas fire gusting warm breath against our legs as we worked opposite each other, threading beads.

5. 'Into the Mystic' – Van Morrison

'Shall we think about moving?' Shuna had sat up, was checking the time on her phone. 'It's getting on.' I nodded, still writing.

6. 'Blowing in the Wind' – Bob Dylan.

'You having fun there?' Shuna asked. I nodded again. 'I'm writing a playlist for Mum, the music I remember her listening to. What's the Dylan song that goes *see for me that her hair's hanging down*?

'"Girl from the North Country", I think.' Shuna replied. I wrote it down and put my notebook back in my pocket and we set off along the beach, song lyrics looping through my head. I made a mental note to add Édith Piaf's 'Je ne Regrette Rien' to the list later.

Two men and a dog were lying under the dunes. The dog, some kind of setter or pointer, bounded up to us. It turned out his owner worked for the North Harris Trust. 'We're waiting for the tide to go out a bit so we can surf,' he explained to us. We chatted for a while. He was passionate about his job and passionate about this place, and his eyes lit up when we outlined the route we were planning to ride over the next few days.

'Are there any locked gates? Do we need to contact anyone?' I asked.

'No, it's all North Harris Trust land, but you'll be spotted. You'll definitely be spotted. There's a watcher's house out there, you know, for the poachers. Someone will see you, even if you don't see them.' We rode away, warmed by this man's enthusiasm and the sun that was now fully out on Sgarasta Bay.

It was early evening when we arrived at Horgabost. 'So where is the croft exactly?' asked Shuna as we stopped in front of a sign that said *Horgabost Township*, the turn-off where Peter had dropped us the evening before.

'I've no idea,' I said, 'but I'm guessing it's up that road somewhere. I'll ask at this house where Iain's croft is.' Iain was the father of my daughter's friend, Corina, whom she shared a room with at Plockton. Iain lived on the mainland but still had a croft here on Harris. His instructions had been 'just turn up and camp'.

A lady came to the door, introducing herself as Mary, and yes, she knew Iain's croft. 'Up there, on the right, there's a house off from the road, a wee black shed below it. That's his croft there, his fields are on either side of the road, they'll be glad of it,' she said, nodding warmly towards the ponies.

We opted for the field below the road. The grass was good, the fences were pony-proof and there were trees, a stand of beautiful Scots Pines. We set up the tent in record time and walked up the road looking for Peter's 'grey house on the right'. Over the next couple of hours he spoilt us with food and wine and kind company. The evening affirmed my growing sense of what a small world it was and how connected we all were. Peter had met Anna-Wendy at his poetry class on North Uist run by the poet Pauline Prior-Pitt. He also knew my daughter's friend Corina through the music scene on Harris. He had moved up a few years earlier, and had clearly made a big effort to integrate, but as he said, 'it's hard here on your own.'

I got the feeling that perhaps he was wondering if he was in the right place. As much as he loved it, it was very remote. He talked about his trips back to London, and the South American band he played in, a tribute band for Victor Jara, the Chilean poet, singer-songwriter and political activist. Peter himself was politically active and we left full of admiration for his involvement in the world, his deep humanitarian caring.

As we got into the tent I was aware of the hot sting on my face and lips from a day spent in the wind, and the warm inner buzz of wine. I felt glad of so many things: glad of Shuna's company, our sharing; glad as I got into my sleeping bag with all my clothes on, including coat and buff, of the runrig providing a smidgen of shelter from the easterly; glad of that same cold easterly keeping the midges away. Listening to the wind soughing in the treetops, I reached my hand down to my left ankle, pictured the small tattoo there, a Scots Pine cone. That mighty pioneer tree which thrives in inhospitable environments and provides habitat for a myriad of other species. *Yes*, I thought as I was falling asleep, *those enduring pines out there are a good sign.*

DAY SEVENTEEN
Horgabost to Aird Asaig

Lifting up onto my elbows I moved aside the tent flap. There was no sight or sound of Shuna. The turf outside was bone dry. Tufts of wool lay caught on the grass sward. Over the lip of the runrig Ross and Chief were standing nose to tail under a bright blue sky. Behind them on the hillside Iain's cream-painted croft house was lit up in early sun. Even the black tin sheds on the roadside had a lustre to them this morning. I stood up and stretched, feeling refreshed. Peter's car was coming down the road, off to catch the early boat to Uist for his monthly poetry class. I stood watching until it turned onto the main road by the house we'd stopped at the night before. He had told us that Mary and Donald MacDonald at the bottom of the road had been very good to him, and suggested we stop off and say a proper hello, and that we were to have a look at the standing stones in their garden.

There was something about his involvement in the world that reminded me of Mum, but without her hardened edges. I remembered a conversation I'd had that January with my school friends, Tiffy and Ros. We'd been on our way back from a few days in Sutherland and stopped at Ardvreck Castle. We'd lain on the bleached winter grass above Loch Assynt, tucking ourselves out of the bitter wind.

'I remember your mum's beauty and glamour,' said Tiffy, 'and her quickness. Her intellectual ability and how she was so connected to the world.'

'Yeah,' I said, 'all that travelling, reading, all that listening to Radio 4, she was on it.'

'But she didn't like me,' said Tiffy. 'She didn't seem to like anyone. She was always so…defiant!'

'She was much braver than I am,' I said, putting my hand on the trunk of a tiny Rowan growing out of the rock face below me.

'Why do the trees like to grow on the steep bit like that?' asked Tiffy.

'It's just that the Sheep and Deer can't eat them there, it's the only place they can survive.'

'Defiance isn't the same as courage,' said Ros from her spot along the bank. 'Whether you're compliant or defiant you're still in thrall. It might look like courage but you're in something's power.'

'That sort of makes sense,' said Tiffy. 'There was a giggly girlishness to Kathryn, wasn't there? And she was so petulant sometimes, childish, always had to sit at the head of the table, make other people do things for her. Do you remember the teaspoon thing?' Tiffy burst out laughing. 'She'd make you or Tom get up and walk all the way round to the drawer to get her a teaspoon when the drawer was right beside her!'

'From what you've told us, Beady, she never had her needs met as a little girl. If you let go of being a child, you're letting go of ever being parented,' said Ros.

I felt an ache in my chest as I watched wind-dolphins skim across the loch.

'I read an article about taking all the good things you got

from your parents and laying down the rest,' Ros said.

'Sound advice,' replied Tiffy. 'Sometimes it's not easy though.'

Wind-ruffled Chickens scattered across the field outside No 6 Horgabost, Mary and Donald's house. Donald was delighted to show us the standing stones. Shuna and I took it in turns to go and look, while the other held the ponies and chatted with Mary. The garden was a mass of colour. Tiny Lettuces grew in neat rows, Lupins reached tall in crimsons and pinks and yellows. There were banks of wild Geraniums, and half-feral Cats appearing and disappearing so shyly, silently, you wondered if they were real.

'At one time there were seven stones around the main cap stone, two metres tall, they say.' Donald was pointing to the remains of Coire na Feinne chambered cairn. The tumble of stones was encircled by hedges and flower beds. 'They burned bodies and put the ashes inside. We had students out here, studying it all. Down the road is the MacLeod stone, it's very large that one. At the equinox the sun sets directly in line with the stone and St Kilda. It was also a clock. At one time there were twelve stones around it, they say, and depending where the sun was the shadows would fall on the right time of day.'

After we'd both seen the stones the four of us stood chatting in the sunshine.

'I remember all the working ponies at Sgarasta,' said Donald, 'there were lots of them at one time.'

'Are you both from here?'

'I'm from the east side,' said Mary, 'so is Donald originally but his parents came here in 1937.'

'I was six and a half,' he said. I did a quick sum in my head, that would put him in his eighties, hard to believe with his broad upright stance and more hair on his head than a lot of men half his age.

'My father and my grandfather built this house together,' he continued. 'They took stones from the hill and built it. You see, crofts came available here, the Ministry of Agriculture bought land off what was then a single estate. You were awarded a croft, and a £150 loan, and were given one hundred years to pay it off at 300 per cent interest. See this road here?' Donald pointed up the township road. 'My father helped build it, he was paid £1.50 a week. He paid off every penny of that loan in a lot less than a hundred years. So, where are you two riding today?'

'We're going over the Coffin Route to the other side.'

'That's a good path. A strong path.'

'They used to bring the bodies east to west,' said Mary.

'Why was that?'

She looked at me, a stir of humour in her eyes. 'Because it's hard to dig a grave in rock.'

We said our goodbyes and rode onto the machair, past a set of rusting harrows, and the campsite, and onto the beach. Both Peter last night, and the Macleods this morning, had bemoaned the existence of the campsite, how it had changed the place and was damaging the machair. 'Our view's a very different one nowadays to what it was,' Mary had said.

We avoided the tents and rode onto pristine tide-swept sand. 'We're so lucky with the weather, seeing these beaches in this light,' said Shuna. We carried on around the coast to Seilebost. The tide was well out and a vast triangle of rose-gold sand opened up to the east. To the north we could see a stripe of white that was Luskentyre beach, and between here and there foam-finned waves chased each other. Sheep were graze-drifting on the machair, their keel marks the same turquoise as the sea behind them. Further along we saw a metal trolley down by the shore. It had a wooden-handled rake and a green plastic bucket resting on it, and parked nearby, belly down, was a wheelbarrow.

Then we came to the orange and red netting bags, eight of

them, there on the roadside, all full to bursting with freshly collected Cockles. Someone, or some few, had been busy this morning. All those sea creatures inside their hinged heart-shaped shells. I thought of Mum's shell collection, still in boxes, each treasure wrapped carefully in newspaper: Wentletrap, Horse Conch, Scotch Bonnet, Moon Snail, Angel Wings. Many of these shells Mum had collected along tidelines in West Africa. *Never buy shells*, she used to say, *people kill the creatures for their shells, only take what you find already empty on the beach.*

We stopped to let the ponies graze by the wooden sign that said *Frith-Rathad, The Harris walkway*, at the start of the Coffin Route. A postie stopped in his van to say hello, he was delighted to see the ponies. Shortly afterwards two cyclists stopped, Highland pony enthusiasts form Norfolk. We talked pony types and colours and feet and feed and miles and temperaments before carrying on, warmed by the chat but longing for quiet again. By a rusting tin sheep fank we ate our lunch, a Golden Eagle circling overhead, the first we'd seen on our trip. With the bright sea behind us, we were heading into rock and hill and cloud.

As the track rose higher the rain came on. It felt strange to be on a hill track after all that machair, to hear the scrabble of stone underfoot. Once through the pass the track began to descend. I put Ross's rope over his saddle and let him follow me freely, that way he was better able to see where to put his feet. As Donnie had said, the track was good and strong. A lot of work had been put into it recently: new paving through boggy patches and stone bridges across ditches. It was a real pleasure to follow an ancient path that was still being maintained. Behind me Ross steadily picked his way, and behind him followed Shuna and Chief. Shuna was still riding, hands in pockets, chin tucked in, hood up against the rain and wind. A thin metallic measure of sea appeared through the cloud ahead. So many tones of grey in this place: the rocks ratcheting up the hillsides on either side of me; the layered sky; the pooling Lichens; the silver-grey dead-wood of the Heather. And then a startle of deep red, a Wren, so close I could see the dark strip at its eye, the banded-ripple of its tiny tail. Then it was gone, a quivering figment in my mind's eye.

I waited by a burn for the others to catch up. It was an ideal place to fill water bottles; natural shelves in the hillside made a series of water fountains. Listening to the water chuntering its downward journey, I could see the path trickling like molten-solder towards the sea. It was a good spot, there was something about it. The ponies thought so too. When Chief arrived they both began eating the peat, great fibrous mouth-fuls of it, that must have been rich in some mineral they were needing.

The path joined the road at the head of Loch Stockinish. We were on The Golden Road once again, and just a few hundred yards up the road was The Bays Café we'd driven past yesterday. Back in the hostel in Leverburgh the St Kilda couple had told us that we must stop off there for tea and cake. They described their long chats with the two ladies who worked there, Anne and Jessie, and the delicious baking for sale. The sign said 'Closed'.

'But it's Saturday,' said Shuna. We'd both been really looking forward to a cup of tea, some cake, and meeting those legendary ladies. The Bays Café was only open Monday to Friday it turned out, weekends off for Anne and Jessie, and who could blame them? Half an hour later, after a steep climb, we were within sight of the main road and the pickup. The sun came out and we stepped off the road onto a rise where there was a smattering of grass. Letting Chief and Ross graze we stood and stared out. The sun changed everything. Nearby hill lochs reflected blue between shivers of green reeds. Boat-sized boulders laid graphite shine across the landscape. A lamb, lying next to its mother, was impossibly white.

We loaded the ponies and drove towards Tarbert, having decided to avoid riding on the fast and busy main road unless we absolutely had to. We were staying with Katie Ann, Corina's mum, in Tarbert that night. The ponies would stay further on in a small settlement called Aird Asaig on the west coast of North Harris. Ruari in Leverburgh had kindly put us in touch with his friend Kenny who had offered us a field. Kenny and his family gave us an enthusiastic welcome, and while Shuna was chatting to Kenny his daughter Bella took me to meet her pony 'Laney'. We made plans for Bella and her friend and their two ponies to join us on the first part of the ride the next day.

'It won't do her any harm to miss church for once,' Kenny said, 'they've been following you on Facebook, it's great for them to get a chance to ride with different folks.'

'What lovely people,' I said, as we drove away.

'Kenny told me a terrible story,' Shuna said, 'about the last working horse being taken off the croft here. He was four years old, the horse belonged to his grandfather, but they'd got a tractor and the horse was no longer needed. He can remember them trying to put the horse in the trailer to go away. He remembers crying and that the horse didn't want to go, that it took a long time to load him.' Shuna paused. 'God knows where it went, but that was the last time there was a horse on the croft. Until Bella got her ponies. He loves seeing horses back on the place.'

The minute we stepped into the house on MacQueen Street we were enveloped in warmth and laughter and non-stop chatter. It was wonderful to see Katie Ann. Corina was there too, back from Plockton on study leave, and her younger sister Lauren.

We met 'Jophes', Corina's chinchilla, who had the softest fur I'd ever felt.

'Where does the name "Jophes" come from?' I asked.

'When I was wee my uncle had a hamster called Joseph. I couldn't pronounce it and called him Jophes.' Corina was always laughing. Her *clàrsach*, Celtic harp, was under the window. I felt a pang of longing to see my daughter, also a harp player. We'd been missing each other on the phone. Corina filled me in on how she was. Shuna and I had showers, and afterwards, feeling clean and happy, drank white wine and ate fish and chips. 'We always eat takeaway on a Saturday,' Katie Ann said.

I loved the idea of family rituals. Would it be too late for me to start some now, with the children all in their teens? This was a family's family, and it made me long to see my own. Corina's grandparents and uncles lived on the same street. Each other's houses were treated as their own. Katie Ann told heart-warming stories about uncles and aunts and parents and grandparents. About helping the neighbours. About sometimes helping too much.

'I told her not to,' said Corina.

'But I had to,' said Katie Ann.

Once I was in bed, away from the warm hullabaloo of this family, the worry I'd been keeping away all evening pressed in. Next day's ride into Kinloch Rèasort. The weather wasn't looking good, and there were so many unknowns regarding the route, and camping out there. I realised, being honest with myself, that I had a sense of dread, and there was something else: a niggling feeling that I'd forgotten something. The beads! I hadn't left a bead for Mum today. How could I have forgotten? I thought back over the day. The burn where we filled our water bottles, that would have been the perfect place to leave a bead, dropped into one of those little peaty pools. Or perhaps left resting on top of one of the surrounding boulders hallmarked by glaciers and lichen. Had that burn been a Hebridean tributary of Lethe, the river of oblivion and forgetfulness in Greek mythology? I had forgotten to leave Mum a bead, crossing Harris, her favourite Hebridean island, from west to east. Forgetfulness. Oblivion.

How much of Mum was I forgetting? I could barely recall her voice now. When I heard her talking in my head sometimes the words and intonation were clear, but more often they were jumbled, faded. That intense laugh of hers that had been so 'her', even that I had trouble conjuring now. I thought about her last days of speaking, when the tumour had interrupted her speech and the words burbled incoherently, strange burbling like that burn on the hill today. I imagined what it must have been like for her, in that locked-in state, as language, her sharpest tool, abandoned her. It didn't bear imagining. A fisted ache spread across my chest and I closed my eyes, assuring myself that things would feel better in the morning. Think of another song for her playlist! Hah, yes, 'Suzanne' by Leonard Cohen. She'd loved his music, as I did, *and she feeds you tea and oranges that come all the way from China*. I smiled, remembering the oranges. Mum had been so particular about peeling them, there was 'a right way'. Just as there was 'a right way' of putting the 'lavatory paper' on the holder. One right way for each, and she knew both of them. I couldn't remember either.

DAY EIGHTEEN

Aird Asaig to Kinloch Rèasort

Back at the field the next morning Ross and Chief stood looking down towards the other ponies. Kenny stood with his daughter, her friend Erin and their two ponies Laney and Gucci. The horsebox was already attached to Kenny's black Mitsubishi and there was a whirl of preparation going on.

'We'd better get a move on,' I said to Shuna, 'they look just about ready to go.'

'Let's not rush the packing, we don't know when we'll next meet the pickup. Can you go and get the electric tape out of the boot? We'll cut off that length now.'

We didn't know if there'd be any enclosure out at Kinloch Rèasort so were taking tape with us. Both ponies were wary enough of electric fencing for us not to need a battery pack. Sitting alongside our concerns was our mutual excitement about heading into the wilds to a place that was, by all accounts, 'out of this world'. 'Morning all,' said Kenny, winding down his window and coming to a stop in front of us. 'We'll just go on ahead and get ourselves sorted out and see you over there. You know where you're going don't you? You'll see the horsebox anyway. There's a car park there for the birders so should be plenty of room to park. See you shortly then.' We'd arranged to box the few road miles along the north side of Loch Siar to the start of the track towards Kinloch Rèasort.

'You can feel the rain coming, can't you?' said Shuna as we pulled away.

'That must be the old Whaling Station,' I said, pointing to a brick chimney in the bay below us. 'Maybe we can check it out when we come back to get the pickup.' I shuddered, imagining the water below mordant red with Whale blood. I was also intrigued. At one time whaling had been an important part of the economy and culture here, and the slipway and a single brick chimney was all that was left. In *Poacher's Pilgrimage* an aged local resident is quoted as remembering how in the 1920s 'steam-powered whalers heaved into the bay with up to three carcasses at a time being towed behind (...) the smell was like the Devil's kitchen; yet nothing could make leather softer, nothing burn a lamp's flame brighter, than pure sperm oil'.

Twenty winding minutes later we parked alongside the sign that said *Eagle Observatory 2km*. There were several cars parked, and a steady trail of walkers dotted the glen.

'Popular spot this,' I said to Kenny as he came towards us.

'Aye, there'll be a few people on the track to the observatory, but after that you won't see many people. Shall we head back now?' he asked, looking at Shuna. They'd arranged that she'd drive her pickup and box back to Aird Asaig and he'd bring her back. It would be a lot easier if we were hitchhiking to get a lift back to Aird Asaig, which was on the main road to Stornoway, than to get a lift out here.

While I waited for Shuna and Kenny I put the ponies' hoof boots on, checked the wires were secure, the Velcro straps snugly closed. I put the saddles on, then the saddlebags, heavier today with all the camping gear. Ross and Chief stood looking brightly towards the other ponies from where they were tied to a padlocked gate. It struck me then, that although locked gates were a common enough site on the mainland, it was the first I'd seen on this trip. Kenny said he'd got a loan of the key so that he could drive on up the glen and be there in case the girls needed him during our ride. I was touched by his fatherly care.

Shuna and I followed the girls whose ponies were setting a fast pace. We rode past an enclosure that had been planted with native trees and crossed a brand-new bridge, everything was smart and well maintained.

'Great to see the tree plantings,' I said. A sound drifted across the boggy moorland on our right, a clear ringing triple-call that I'd never heard before. We both stopped. I could see a wading-type bird with a long beak, its underparts white. Some walkers were coming towards us, led by a stocky-legged woman with an expensive-looking pair of binoculars around her neck. 'Do you know what that bird is?' I asked her.

Without lifting her binoculars she said confidently, 'It's a Greenshank, we saw it on the way up.' I smiled my thanks. It was the first time I'd ever seen a Greenshank, a bird, like the Redshank, associated in Gaelic culture with the liminal space between worlds. We passed the eagle observatory, a quirky wooden building with a glass front. Then the rain came on. The wind was barrelling up the glen throwing it hard against our backs. After an hour or so we met up with Kenny. He decided the girls and the ponies could go back now, the return trip might well feel longer as they'd be riding into the rain, and they were already wet, but happy. We shared the last of our mint Kit Kats with them and said our goodbyes.

It was well past lunchtime when Loch Bhoishimid came into sight, and my heart lifted when I saw the newly built fishing bothy: wooden clad and flat roofed. Perhaps we'd be able to shelter inside for a while. A cold wetness started to seep in at the base of my neck and down the backs of my legs. I turned around in the saddle to see if Shuna had seen the bothy, but she and Chief both had their heads down. My friend, head-to-toe in waterproofs, was as dark as the steep face of Sròn Ard which rose almost vertically behind her. It was a shock, suddenly being in the shadow of these hills and the thick furrows of raincloud. Chief, and the slate-silver track he was walking on, offered the only brightness in that rain-blackened glen. I followed the curves of the track back towards Loch a Siar, now just a thin chink in the distance.

The bothy was padlocked but along the glass front that faced the loch was a bench. It was sheltered there in the lee of the wind, and we got out the gas stove and made a strong coffee. Then another. Under the bench were stacks of offcuts from the cladding, bright and dry and smelling comfortingly of freshly sawed wood, of the log-pile at home. In near silence we watched the water dripping down the ponies' flanks, running in rivulets off their muzzles, their manes, the loops in the lead ropes. They stood tied to a fence, motionless and resigned to the rain, while we felt the caffeine kicking into our bloodstream. Faraway light licked the skyline, a wave of brightness swept across the loch and suddenly the ponies' wet faces were gleaming in full sunshine.

'I've got a shitload of stuff in here.' Shuna was packing away the stove in her saddlebags, and I heard in her tone the nervousness we were both feeling. Shortly, the track would come to an end and we'd have some potentially very tricky kilometres, with no path, to navigate before reaching the head of Loch Rèasort. I silently questioned the wisdom of abandoning the original plan of sticking to tracks and roads on the east side of Harris. But I was already bewitched by this place, drawn towards those lines on the map that looked like the head of a water horse, *each-uisge* in Gaelic. Its tongue, the river marking the boundary between Harris and Lewis. One meaning of Loch Rèasort is 'division fjord'. We both felt a powerful pull to go into the heart of this land mass, to the remote abandoned settlement at the head of the loch, and hopefully to continue north to the road that would take us to the standing stones at Callanish. That was our plan A, while plan B was, 'If it gets too difficult, we'll turn back.'

'It's rough, but at least the ground is firm,' I called over my shoulder. Ross was doing a magnificent job of helping me pick the route. I was respectful of the knowledge that ran deep in his blood. We were keeping high up on the shoulder of the hill where the grass was long and tussocky and hadn't been grazed by sheep for years, if ever. Deer were here though, and I felt a rush of gratitude every time we picked up one of their narrow weaving paths, noticeable by the golden colour of last year's trampled Molinia grass, and the scatterings of their droppings. We stopped to catch our breath while water flickered like minnows amongst the dunlins and peat hags below.

'I'm glad we're up here, we did the right thing to stay high.' Stating the obvious is something I do when nervous. Over the next two hours we inched our way round the side of the hill. As the crow flies it was hardly more than a kilometre, but at the pace we were going it felt like ten. We picked our way through piles of stones tangled through with Moss and aged Heather, and ridden with hidden holes, *leg-breaking holes*. My thoughts were getting darker.

'Look, the Deer,' shouted Shuna. Away down below us I saw them and automatically started to count, seven, a good sign. They floated up the hillside in a soundless curve, much lighter than the Deer we were used to seeing in Argyll. Less red, more of a silver sandy colour, *like moth wings* I was thinking, when Ross stumbled behind me, his front hoof catching my right ankle. Pain burned and, for a white-hot moment, I wondered if my ankle was broken, but already I'd taken the next step and it was weight bearing and therefore okay.

Here the ground was more level, but the glen floor below was as disarrayed and mired as my thoughts were becoming.

Pain, adrenalin and lack of food were taking their toll. *Breathe, Beady*. Two Ravens flew below us, dropping vocables into the brightening afternoon, so close I could hear the air shush past the tips of their primary feathers. They landed up ahead. As we approached the pair took off in a clamour of discordant protest from their treasure, a half-eaten Deer carcass. Past the stripped bones, I knew I had to watch my thoughts as closely as I was watching where I was putting my feet. The resin-sweet smell of decaying flesh followed us.

I turned around to warn Shuna but she'd already spotted the carcass and was stepping around it. Behind her I could still see Loch Bhoishimid, where in 1912, while fishing this loch, JM Barrie got the inspiration to write his play 'Mary Rose', in which he explored the effects of war on a child's subconscious. In these quiet days of riding I'd reached a new understanding of how a different kind of war, my parent's divorce, was still affecting my own subconscious after all these years. I had also gained a fuller appreciation of how the things closest to my heart were gifts they had both given me: a love of Birds, wildlife and the outdoors from Dad; a love of Horses and literature from Mum; a love of Scotland from each of them. To them both I owed this feeling of belonging in Scotland that didn't, some would say, fit with my accent, or my birthplace, but that I knew perfectly fitted the shape of my soul.

Three hours and two kilometres after leaving the fishing bothy we reached the dip on the skyline that the seven Deer had disappeared through. We were now on the ridge that ran from the top of the hill we'd been traversing, Cearascleit Mhor, down to the top of Cearascleit Beag. According to the map we'd get a good view from there as far as Loch Rèasort. We felt light-headed and light-hearted as the sun reappeared and glanced off the pale rocks all around us. The late afternoon promised to be a stunner. I'd been saying out loud at regular intervals, 'We can always go back,' but it had been a tough few hours and the thought of having to return as we had come wasn't appealing. We were being pulled onwards. We picked the stoniest route towards the nose of Cearascleit Bheag. Broad patches of fiercely weathered bedrock felt impervious underfoot, the ponies blew appreciatively. A landscape opened to the north and east as far as we could see. My heart sank. It was brown, very brown, and scored with dark lines showing us that it was peat hags, miles of peat hags, that lay between us and the stone-happed hills to the north east. According to the map it was in these hills that we'd pick up the old postal route. But perhaps there'd be another route out. I brought my gaze closer in, there were two rivers below us, both meandering their way towards the same oval of water.

'Look! That must be Loch Rèasort, and there's a shieling.' I looked to where Shuna was pointing. The straight lines of the faraway building, its pale roof, the different tone of green where animals had grazed, sent a thrill through the two of us.

'I think it'll be fine. We can get down to the river from here, and then follow it to the loch. The riverbanks look good.' I nodded in agreement, both of us in denial of the 'going on regardless' mist that had descended in our adrenalin-kindled minds and bodies.

It had been eight hours since our breakfast in Tarbert, the most delicious bacon and egg rolls we'd ever had. When we'd told Katie Ann she'd answered, 'That's because the rolls are from Stag's Bakery in Stornoway, they're the best.' I'd had a feeling it was her generous heart that had been the magic ingredient though. We stopped on the nose of the hill and I poured the sardine oil into the rough grass. *For the faeries*, I thought to myself, as I now did every time I drained a can of sardines or smoked mussels into the ground. Adrenalin had taken away my appetite and the oatcakes and sardines were hard to swallow. I wondered, sitting there, how it had been for Mum choking on the least-tiny bit of food, in the

217

end not even being able to suck on a piece of chocolate. She had so loved her food. I looked at the rocks above me. This was a scraped-bare place. I remembered the cold day my brothers and I took Mum's ashes up to the top of *Deadh Choimhead* (meaning Good View), a hill in Glen Lonan that is visible from our three homes. I remembered the wind that day, how it had blown her ashes back against us, into our eyes, our hair, our mouths. I forced myself to think of something else, to focus on the skyline as I swallowed each dry mouthful of my late lunch.

It was an easy enough scramble down to the river. The banks were green and firm, grazed by Deer. The river was scallop-edged with buff sand. In some places, where the pools were darkest, you could see how the water had cut in under the overhanging peat. And then I saw it, there in the grass and heather, a perfect circle of low stone wall, the remains of a beehive dwelling, and a second, and a third. I hadn't realised it at the time but the beehive huts that Alastair McIntosh describes in *Poacher's Pilgrimage* were just over a kilo-metre to the east of where we now were. It was his vivid descrip-tions of how dangerous the ground was in this part of Harris that had originally made me rule out this whole west coast as a possible route. I had forgotten all of that, hadn't connected the two places. Afterwards I'd wonder if it was my subconscious that had drawn me there, knowing this place had something to teach me.

Leaving the ponies to graze on the harlequin-green grass, we went and sat down inside the closest beehive dwelling, our backs to the Lichen-mapped walls. On top of the stones was a thick cushion of Heather, its edge sculpted round and smooth by the weather. 'How lucky are we,' I said, smiling across to a very tired but contented-looking Shuna in the melting evening sunshine. The river bent around us singing over pink gravel shallows. Kenny had told us that this river, Abhainn Mhor, was famous for its Salmon and Sea Trout runs. I could picture the fish now, silver from the sea, following their noses upstream, finning in pools made dark by peat. I took the bead purse out of my pocket. Mum had been, in her own words, 'a culture vulture', with a lifelong passion for archaeology and ancient civilisation, so many passions. I chose a bright red glass bead for the beehive dwelling. *Red for love*, I said quietly as I laid it amongst the Heather branches. *And red for danger*.

We set off down the river leaving the bead behind, shining, the red in the glass picking up the blush at the tips of the new Heather shoots. We lost count of how many times we crossed that river. The Deer, in Gaelic 'crodh-sìth', cattle of the faeries, were still guiding us with their hoof slots in the sandy crossing places. They had mapped the firmest parts of the riverbanks for us, but as we got closer to Loch Rèasort the green riverside turned to treacle-coloured peat that collapsed under foot and hoof, and the trails of heart-shaped hoof prints disappeared. We had to walk long stretches in the river itself, up to our knees in places, the ponies treading gingerly over slippery stones. By now we all smelt of river.

Soon we were in the open at the head of Loch Rèasort, breathing in the salty air lifting off the tidal flats, while the Oystercatchers trailed orange-beaked calls in the last light. We were standing in Lewis now, on cropped grass in front of the house we'd seen from the hilltop. Its tin roof was an ethereal duck-egg blue. Starlings hopped on the chimney breasts, their young croaking coarsely from pitchy nesting places. We walked around to the back of the house where the windows and door-ways were filled in with boulders. Stone walls funnelled into the side of the house, a sort of sheep fank we guessed. The walls had incorporated faces of blue-grey bedrock. At the front of the house were two windows looking out across the river mouth and head of the loch. The tide was low and wet shingle shone orange beyond the river. This must be the 'watcher's cottage' we'd heard about, where estate workers from Amhuinnsuidhe Estate came to keep an eye out for poachers. Even though the land was now community owned by the North Harris Trust, the fishing and sporting rights were still privately owned.

As remote as we were, evidence of humans was everywhere: in the blue-keeled sheep; this boulder-blinded building; the white cottage across the river; the stone ruins of black houses reaching out to the west. There was another river that flowed into the loch just beyond the one we'd followed in. This second river was noisy, we could hear it collecting in invisible pools higher up, then spilling over rocky shelves in an expressive water-led 'yes', over and over again.

'D'you see that fence?' I said, pointing over the bay. 'I'll go across and check if it's an enclosure we could put the ponies in, maybe we could camp over there too.' Relief washed over me as I waded across the river. The low-angled sun dispersed a green sheen through the shallows; a band of weed grew there, perhaps it marked the line between saltwater and fresh water. I stepped out and headed across the gritty sand towards the stone ruins and the fence line, crunching over large blue Mussel shells. Water oozed from my boots. We were in luck, the fence was in good repair, the ponies would have a big field for the night. Even more incredibly there was good grass. We'd already worked out that if we camped on that side of the bay we'd get the morning sun. I waved and shouted back across to Shuna, indicating for her to bring the ponies over. A Sea Eagle flew low and slow directly between us, so close I could see the sharp closing angle of her yellow beak. I shouted and waved again, pointing at the bird, but Shuna was already busy leading the ponies down the narrow stone-cut steps to the river.

While I was waiting, I wandered across to the other house. I read later that these houses, one on Lewis and this one on Harris, were 'white houses' originally built for the estate gamekeepers to live in. They were the only two buildings still with roofs on. The whitewash of their walls was now barely discernible, although the front wall of this one had been redone more recently. By the padlocked door there was a hand-painted sign *Welcome to the last resort. You will never leave.* I smiled, walked on past a verdigris tap attached to a post, and towards two old cast-iron gateposts. There was no fence left, no gate, just these two posts, framing in bright rust the hills we'd come through earlier. I felt so glad we'd made it to this place. I turned and walked back towards the remains of the black houses, and dear Shuna, and the weary magnificent ponies.

'Bloody lucky us!' Shuna said, as we finished the last of our chicken curry and Lidl's tinned aubergines. We both laughed. The ponies looked up at us, stalks hanging from their lips. They dropped their heads again. A breeze was keeping the midges away, we were being so well looked after. We'd been told you could get 'a good feed' of Mussels in this place, but even though the tide was out, we decided to leave the Mussels to themselves, and to the Birds and Otters. We had so much already.

'This is the life,' I said, rubbing my bare feet, which were slowly warming now they were rid of the sodden socks and boots. Just then the Sea Eagle did another fly-by, leaving a startle of bird calls in its astronomical wake; it seemed it was us she had in her inquisitive sights though, not dinner. Then we saw the rainbow, a broad bright thumbs-up of a rainbow, over towards where we hoped to pick up the postal track the next day – good omens all round. We were still spellbound when we lay down inside the tent on the mossy footprint of a black house. We fell asleep quickly, blissfully unaware of how much a place can change in just twenty-four hours, or that we'd be forced to stay another night out there, in the house with stone-filled windows. That second night the words *Welcome to the last resort. You will never leave* would take on a whole other meaning.

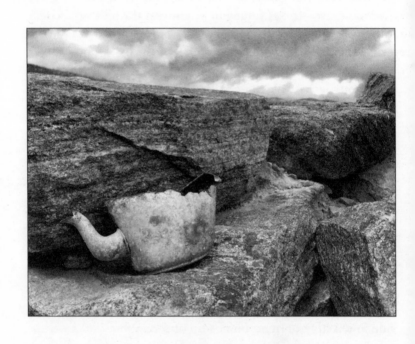

DAY NINETEEN
Kinloch Rèasort

The ricochet-call of a Red Grouse woke me, punctuating sleep-soft memories of other sounds during the night: Snipe drumming overhead; water unspooling in the rivers; the tide hesitating between rocky shores; a high bird call I didn't recognise; the ponies treading by. Even before I opened my eyes I felt the brightness and warmth of a sun already high in the sky. I could hear the comforting sounds of Shuna moving around up behind the tent. I felt deeply rested, in fact, I felt great.

'Ready for porridge?' asked Shuna as I walked towards her. The stove was on, water was boiling and breakfast supplies were laid out; zip-seal bags full of oats and coffee, a wedge of cheese, a small tub of honey. The ponies were lying side by side in exactly the same position, they were doing everything in tandem now; sleeping, peeing, even sighing and blowing was done in sync.

'I'm starving,' I said, my bare feet sinking into the deep moss. 'What a morning, what a spot, this must be one of the most beautiful places on earth.'

'Pretty damn perfect,' Shuna replied as she killed the steam in the pan with a handful of dry oats.

'The ponies were both standing when I got up, they don't

seem any worse for wear after yesterday,' she said. 'Incredible really.' I nodded. They'd had some bad moments yesterday, sinking into peaty riverbanks studded with boulders that could maim a muscle or a tendon if caught wrong.

After breakfast I put on my socks and boots, still soaking from the night before, and went for a wander with my camera. Heading back towards the 'whitehouse' on this side of the bay, I stopped to watch lambs racing along the edges of banks. They were strong-looking, their mothers too . It was a grass-haven for sheep out here in the middle of all those thousands of hectares of peat. The sheep had been clipped last summer, no roughies: sheep that have gone unclipped and are carrying multiple years of fleece-growth. These were well-tended sheep. I stopped by the walls of a ruin. Inside was a carpet of bed springs, old fridges, plastic plates, fishing buoys, rusted tin cans. Outside on the grass was a cream-coloured aluminium jug, its soft lines curved like a sleeping duck. The whole of its base had rotted away. Placing it on a stone windowsill, I stood back to admire it, and looked beyond across the bay towards the duck-egg-blue roof, and the runrigs that rippled down to the shore in the morning light. Shuna looked up from the map as I approached. 'Shall we do a recce without the ponies to see if we can find a way to the Mhorsgail postal route?' she said. 'According to the map it's not far from the house over there,' she said, pointing across the bay.

'Good idea,' I replied. 'I'd love to walk up that other river.' I traced with my finger the blue line that ran to a big pencilled-in oval where Ruari had told us the beehive dwellings were. I clumsily read out the name of the river, 'Abhainn à Clàr Beag.'

'Great,' said Shuna, 'let's get a move on then, we don't want to be leaving too late with the ponies, who knows what the old postal route will be like.'

We took down the tent, repacked the saddlebags, and left

everything in a neat pile before heading back across the bay. 'Back soon,' we told Ross and Chief. We had to ford the river again, this time noticing the remains of a stone bridge that would have given easy access between the settlement of Crola, here on the Harris side of the river, and Luachair on the Lewis side.

From the house we found a good track that went eastwards through a gap in the dyke, the gate long gone. Under the thin turf this was a proper track, but within the next few strides it abruptly ended in peat moor. Just a tiny tantalising stretch of track, something begun and never finished. We checked our bearings on the map and began to pick our way across the moor. It was peat as far as we could see, but not like the peat that we were used to on the mainland. This peat chequered the moor neatly in raised plateaus with dry waterways between. It seemed doable to pick our way from one raised bed of peat to the next. The ground felt surprisingly firm, and after ten minutes or so we both agreed we'd give it a cautionary go with the ponies. The land rose gradually towards a low-backed hill, *Shèlibridh*, alongside which, according to the map, we'd pick up the old postal path, and then hopefully the going would get easier.

'Let's go and find the beehives,' I said, both of us now feeling more positive about the route out. We followed the river south, its banks rich with the scent of new growth. Bright yellow-green leaves of Butterwort glowed starlike over mossy banks, some were flowering, splashes of violet at the end of bowing stems. This insectivorous plant was thriving out here in the acidic ground. Oil seeped from the peat and a rust-red pool was overlaid with rainbow iridescence. The reeds were also red, iron minerals in the ground here had permeated everything. On a rock were two Damselflies attached end to end, lover-lines of vermillion.

Further along, in a place where the burn converged with two

more, we found a beehive shieling of half a dozen dwellings. Two were on their own little island where spating water had sluiced through the ground between the burns, another had been cleaved in half by a new watercourse. Water was marking time here. The beehives were small round hummocks, about six feet in diameter, crowned in brown heather-wood. At one time they would have been igloo-shaped, stonework all the way to the top and covered in turf, leaving a small hole for the smoke. They were roofless now. I crouched down in one of them, eye-height with Vole holes in the Moss and Heather that covered the curved walls underneath. There were small recesses in the stonework, like cupboards. I put my hand into one, brought out a clear glass bottle rimed with earth. I put my hand back in and touched something that crumbled to the touch, a wafer-thin piece of oxidised tin, food cans from goodness knows how long ago.

I'd find out later that just a few hundred yards south of where we were was another shieling where the beehives were intact, the one that Alastair McIntosh describes as *a vision straight from Middle Earth*. In his book he goes on to quote a 'Captain Thomas of the Royal Navy' who in 1859 wrote about the beehive shielings: *all the natives agree that no-one knows who built them, and that they were not made by the fathers nor grandfathers of persons now living*. Captain Thomas on a later visit met the dwelling's summer occupants, three shieling girls who during the day 'minded and milked their cattle' and during the night 'slept inside the ancient shelter, just as their sisters before them had always done'.

I sat on a bed of dried sheep droppings, the walls obviously a favoured shelter spot for them. I reached into my pocket for the bead purse and took out three, one for each of my children. I chose three ceramic glazed beads, one bronze, one terracotta and one royal blue. I threaded them together onto a single string, I didn't want them to become separated. They sat on the curve of the beehive, their sheen picking up the yellow of the Tormentil flowers threading up between the Mosses. I placed the beads in the earthy darkness of the recess. Maybe, I thought, Brèagha, Finn and Oran will come here one day. I liked that thought.

We led Chief and Ross through the gate. Nearby were the long-abandoned blackhouse ruins where the night before we'd stowed the saddles under stone lintels. We tacked up while the ponies grazed the short sweet grass growing along the top of the blackhouse walls. Thick-shelled blue mussels and white cockles were scattered there, it was clearly favoured by birds as a feeding spot. Alongside the houses swept an ancient Goat Willow, its thick trunk spreading perpendicular to the ground, while new shoots sprouted upwards. The tree seemed to hold the heart of the place within its reaches, and between its branches somebody had made a tin-covered shelter, a wooden bench. Behind the tree was a disused sheep dip, a 45-gallon drum lying beside it, rusted away save for one side, and the rim, a perfect circle remaining. So many outlines here, spaces to fill with imaginings of all that had been and gone in this place. I took out a large obsidian bead, black with silver veins, and tied it firmly amongst the silver-green willow leaves.

We left with smiles, and in sunshine, but already we could see a deep bank of clouds coming in. We needed to get a move on. We had no intention of riding as we would need to be close to the ground to read it, and the ponies could do without carrying any extra weight. Crossing the river we walked past the house with its duck-egg-blue roof and up the little spur road to nowhere. Then we began to carefully pick our way east through the patchwork of peat. It was going well, there was movement in the ground, but it was dry and firm on each separate peat plateau. Ross was taking his time, treading carefully, using his nose as

I'd seen him countless times before on wet and peaty ground. I was in front and Chief and Shuna followed behind. With hindsight I think there had been a hesitation, a cautionary feeling from Ross behind me, but it all happened so fast. I'd crossed the ground between two peat plateaus, he followed, and there it was, the unmistakable grunt of distress. I spun round and his hindquarters were in deep, he'd broken the surface of what I'd just walked across, what I'd thought was fine and firm. He scoured for purchase with his front hooves but only succeeded in spinning his front end round, away from the dry ground I was on. He was floundering. I had a sense of looking down on the scene from far away, *this can't actually be happening*.

'Beady!' shouted Shuna. 'Don't put any tension in the rope. Leave him be!'

It was his tail I couldn't take my eyes off, spread out behind him in coils across the skulking surface of 7,000 years of peat formation. It was beyond anything I had ever seen, nothing like our previous experiences in peat. I reached across trying to undo his girth straps, succeeded and somehow pushed the saddle over onto the peat on the other side of him. My arms felt watery and weak.

'Okay,' said Shuna. In that one word I heard calm, and I heard a plan. Then Ross started to plunge again, going ever deeper downhill, further into this underground current of peat-hell. The peat hags lifted higher around him.

'Come on, Ross,' I said, trying to angle his head towards the drier ground.

'He needs his head, don't put anything in the rope,' Shuna repeated. Her words finally sunk in. 'Okay, he needs to rest.' She squatted down beside him and reached out her hand, gently stroking his face. 'It's going to be okay,' she said.

Choking back tears, I watched the amber in his eyes darkening in fear.

'He needs to rest. He knows what he's doing, Beady, he's a pro,' she said, willing me to be present. 'He needs to recover his strength for the next try. He'll try again, and we need to make it as easy as possible for him to get out.' At that he heaved again, but he was only sinking deeper. His struggles stopped quicker this time and he lay quiet. Meanwhile Chief stood motionless behind Shuna, we were both acutely aware of the danger Chief was also in.

'Let's try to dig a space around his legs.' We knelt down and scraped away from his forelegs, handful by handful of bituminous black peat. We couldn't reach his hind legs, one of them looked like it was bent back behind him at an unnatural angle. I looked away. We were working furiously now, slowly creating a pocket of air around each of his motionless legs.

'Is he exhausted?' I asked Shuna.

'No, he's resting. I told you, he knows what he needs to do. He knows better than we do. Keep digging.' I finally reached a hoof, curled my fingers around the horn wall.

'Now, we need to find anything we can to put under the hooves that that will give him traction: coats, bags, anything,' said Shuna, standing up. We pulled off his saddlecloth, our coats, waterproof trousers, and packed them as quickly as we could under his hooves. Ross tried again with us both urging him on. 'Come on, Ross, come on, Ross.'

He couldn't shift himself. He just couldn't do it, even with the air pockets around his legs, even with the new traction beneath his hooves. He couldn't get any purchase on the peat. The grip the bog had on his hind legs, the suction on his belly, it was too much. He rested again, his eyes dulling.

We stood in silence. I was doing the sums. Eight hours on foot back the way we came to get a phone signal. God knows how long if one of us carried on to the postal route, so many unknowns there. One of us would have to stay with the ponies.

Where would Chief be safe? How would that be, in the peat, all those hours? What about that hind leg, that angle? Would a helicopter come, how else could he be lifted out? All these thoughts blooming like an oil spill in my mind. *You need to focus, Beady*.

'We have to get this right,' said Shuna. 'I think we only have one more chance. We're going to put more stuff under his hooves. We're going to let him rest. Then I'm going to lead Chief away. We're only going to get one shot at this. I'm hoping seeing his friend leaving will give him the extra impetus he needs.' I nodded. After a few minutes she said, 'Okay, Beady, I'm going to go away now, remember, do NOT pull on his head.' She started to lead Chief away, as best she could, following in our earlier footprints. We knew now that the whole area was treacherous, that we probably couldn't even trust those hoof prints from earlier, but it was the best we had to go on. This Lewis peat was an entirely different beast. Ross was trying, pushing, grunting. *Keep the rope loose*. 'Come on, Ross,' I said out loud. Something was happening, he was moving. He was making headway. He got his front hooves on the plateau that Chief had just left, he heaved and he pushed and with a groan ripping from deep inside him he hauled himself out of that shifting morass of blackness.

'Hold him! Make sure he doesn't fall back!' shouted Shuna.

He was unsteady. I soothed him with words, put my hand on his neck, saw his four hooves on the ground and stemmed back the tears.

Shuna was taking off Chief's saddle. 'We'll come back for the saddles later. We have to get them back on safe ground.' We lost our footprint trail almost immediately but saw the hole in the dyke, the track, and carefully picked our way towards it, step by step, all our senses on high alert. Not until we were standing on that stony track did we allow ourselves to relax, and then the tears came.

'Thank you, Shuna. Thank God for you. Sorry I was so useless.'

'You did great, I can't imagine how I would have felt if it was Chiefy back there. We're not going anywhere else today. We need to get them back to the field, get the maps out, and find another way out of here. Ross needs to rest. He looks fine though. What an amazing horse you are, Ross!' He was standing square, as if it had never happened, but for the peat clinging to his legs, his underbelly, in his tail. The same colour as him, except without the amber that was now back burning in his eyes.

I left Shuna with the ponies grazing by the house and went back for the saddles. We rested by the stone-blinded windows and I remembered the small bottle of Rescue Remedy in my saddlebag and, with still-shaking hands, squeezed drops into Ross's bottom lip. I was in shock, struggling to organise my thoughts, and very, very scared.

'What's that?' said Shuna. I looked across the bay towards where she was pointing. My confused mind couldn't compute what I was seeing. My heart started to race, not in a good way. Battle-ship grey. Boat? Or barge? Barge-boat? Landing craft? Men on deck with binoculars, looking right at us. Navy? I was confused. I was thinking military. Secret. I was thinking war. I was thinking weird.

'It's probably an estate boat,' said Shuna. Yes, that made more sense than the Navy. My mind was scrambled. It wasn't a big boat. 'Maybe they're the watchers we've heard about, coming to check for poachers.' A wave of relief spread through me. Maybe they could help. If they were local they'd know the ground. A way out. Routes. Local knowledge.

'Looks like they're landing on the other side.' The boat lined up alongside the rocks below the willow tree.

We set off across the bay, hopeful, excited to meet these people.

'Shuna, you talk to them, they'll be more friendly with your accent.' I still had this thing, this shame thing around my accent, worry of being pigeonholed, misunderstood. It went way back to school days, being taunted for my English accent.

'Okay,' she said, knowing this wasn't the time to tell me, yet again, that people didn't care about my accent, that I had a lovely voice.

A tall, bearded man, rosy-cheeks, loose-fitting jeans, answered her greeting. 'Thought we were seeing things when we saw the ponies,' he said. 'I could do with a pair of ponies like that to get the deer off the hill.' Okay, I could place him now. A stalker. A friend. Fabulous! I'd been a pony girl in my late teens, carrying deer off the hill with Highland garrons, and was still passionate about the tradition of working ponies in this way.

'What are you all doing here?' I asked him. There was someone with red hair, smart binoculars hanging over checked shirts. I remember that, but was it one pair of binoculars, or several? I could only take in small pictures at a time, still struggling to make sense of things.

'We're from Amhuinnsuidhe Estate, bringing in building supplies for the house over there,' he said, pointing to the white-house this side of the bay.

'It's a three-bedroomed house,' one of the other men said. 'All mod cons.'

'What are you doing out here?' our friend asked.

'We camped here last night, came in from Loch Bhoishimid yesterday.'

'That would have been some tricky ground to cover,' he said. I heard understanding in his words. Yes, these folks got it, hopefully they'd be able to help.

'We were planning to ride north, to connect with the postal path to Morsgail,' Shuna said.

'That path doesn't exist,' somebody said. I was looking at my blackened hands, feeling the shame build like the pressure of the peat under my fingernails. *How had we thought it'd be okay to come out here without doing any proper route planning?*

'One of the ponies got badly bogged, just beyond the house over there.' Shuna nodded over the bay. 'We're staying another night and looking for a better way out.'

'You got bogged that close in?' said the man with red hair. 'It only gets worse after that.'

'Is there another way out?' Shuna asked hopefully.

'We really don't want to go back the way we came in,' I added, picturing those collapsing riverbanks.

'You're in the wettest part of Harris here.' Then he abruptly turned to the others saying, 'Come on, we need to get all this stuff moved before the tide changes.'

'Do you want a hand?' we asked.

'No, don't worry.' There was a long silence. 'But thank you.' It was in that moment that I felt the change in the mood. That I realised help wouldn't be forthcoming, although still I hoped that after they'd got their work done they'd look at the map with us. I'd been holding it all the time, tightly. I wonder, had they noticed our tear-stained faces, wet boots, peat-clagged coats and hands, the blood on Shuna's arms?

The men were suddenly busying around us. Half a dozen of them. Carrying rolls of insulation, plastic-wrapped mattresses. We were invisible. It struck me then, how strange, if these were hillmen, that they weren't more interested in the ponies, in what we were doing. A tight-lippedness descended amongst them and my confidence evaporated.

'Shuna, I need to walk,' I said, knowing she'd understand. 'I'll go along the coast here, check how far the field goes, and see what the ground looks like further on. Maybe there'll be a route out along the coast to the west there. I won't be long, then hopefully we can ask these guys to look at the map with us.'

I walked off, focusing on where I was putting my feet, trying to breathe out the fear locked in my muscles. I passed Ross and Chief, both happily grazing. I walked through the field, giving thanks again for the good fence, the good grass, the comforting sound of calling sheep. All too soon the grass slipped into peat. On foot it was easy to walk across, but I knew that heading this way with the ponies wasn't an option, not if the ground was like this all the way. A memory came back of Ruari saying they'd started to build a path out here from another village further west, but it had been abandoned. At the end of the field was a gateway but no gate in sight. I doubted the ponies would come down this far, they wouldn't want to leave the grass, but just in case I thought I'd better sort something. On the rocky shore I found a length of fishing net and hung it across the gateway. The sight of my hands shocked me, the skin had dried out in the peat, was grained like rhinoceros skin, a thousand wrinkles deep. I walked back, hurrying my steps, I didn't want to miss the men.

Shuna came to meet me and we walked back together, saying very little. We stood near the crew who were finishing up. Nobody was looking our way. Nobody was talking to us. It was as if, in our absence, something had been further decided. We looked at each other in silent recognition of something strange in the air. 'There's the friendly one,' Shuna said quietly, 'coming back from the house. Why don't we try to show him the map before he gets back to the others?'

'Can you just have a quick look at the map with us, please?' we asked. He looked towards the boat uncomfortably.

'Okay, but like they said, there's no easy way out of here. You'll need to go back the way you came, but there's maybe an easier bit I can show you. Here, there's possibly a better way if you follow a different river. Look, the river starts there.' He pointed beyond the white house. 'There's a fisherman's path up the side, you'll get the ponies up fairly easily. Then at this bend in the river,' he pointed at the map, 'cross here, you'll see a shallow gravel bed where the deer cross.'

There was a shout from the barge, he was being called back. 'Look, this is tricky this ground, all of this, but if you pick a route between these knolls you'll get to the hillside, onto harder ground.' We both thanked him. A shrill whistle split the air, like a dog whistle, and he left, with a quiet 'good luck'.

The boat disappeared out of sight at the head of the bay, the sound of its engine fading, and then silence. 'Thank God they've gone,' said Shuna. 'That was so weird.' We could hear Oystercatchers calling, and the sun came out, spilling the afternoon into early evening.

'There was something so strange about them,' I said, 'apart from the friendly guy, but even he went a bit odd.'

'It could be that thing that sometimes happens in groups,' said Shuna. 'Individually they might be lovely, but in a group, you know, if there's one total dickhead, the whole group changes. No offer of us using the house then,' she said with a wry smile. 'Let's go over to the other house and take the stones away from the door. It's not padlocked. Might as well make ourselves as comfortable as possible, we need to get a decent rest tonight. We'll be better off inside if rain is on its way.'

'They must think we're total idiots,' I said.

Shuna looked at me, her blue eyes ice bright. 'Beady, we're out in the middle of nowhere, we're in deep shit. I really don't give a fuck what those guys might think. I can't believe you're even having that thought. We've got far more important things to worry about.' I gave her a steady look back, and burst out laughing.

'You're right. I can't believe I just said that!' All my life I'd worried far too much about what other people thought. Maybe it was time for a change. 'Ross and Chief are fine. All our gear's back at the house, that's handy. I'd really like to walk the route he just showed us on the map. Get a feel for it before we try it with the ponies.'

Shuna nodded. 'Let's go then.'

We walked towards the river, past the house with the new mattresses stashed away inside, past the tap and the empty iron gateposts. I thought of that other gate yesterday. Had it been an omen, that locked gate at the end of the track? Mum's friend Moira told me a story after Mum died. In 1997 they'd both gone to Morocco, 'quite an experience travelling with your mother', she'd said. 'She drove through an armed checkpoint, just put her foot down and said, *fuck it, let's go, I'm not giving them any money*. She was a nightmare, your mum, and wonderful, and totally impossible.' Yes, *fuck it, let's go*, I thought as I stepped in beside Shuna.

We found the fishermen's path and started to follow it. Imagining I had Ross with me, I pictured each and every step we'd make the next morning in my mind's eye. Yes, Shuna's right. Time to stop worrying about what other people think. I'm in my mid-forties. Time to drive through a few armed checkpoints. Poach a few fish. Break a few rules. Meeting the boat, and those men, had been a watershed moment for me. We trod that riverbank imagining ourselves to be half a ton of pony weight, but knowing it would look altogether different in the morning when we had them with us. I looked for fish in the gold-lit water, I saw none: no evening rise, no gash of silver, no belly swaying beneath peaty overhangs. Perhaps they were down in the bay, nosing into the tickle of fresh water, waiting for rain to push them upriver on the next leg of their journey.

'It won't be easy,' I said, 'but he was right, the deer stalker, this is a better route.' Feeling reassured we retraced our steps. In reverse order I engraved every yard of the route we'd take the next day on my mind, each landmark of Deer track, Primrose patch, river rock. I was good at that, remembering a route, footfall by footfall, one area where Shuna could hand over to me. That and my sense of direction. A Red Grouse startled up by our feet, its wingbeats stirring our blood.

'Our welfare is more important than any barred doors,' said Shuna, as we lifted away the stones from the doorway. Inside the house was cold and dark. The windows at the back of the house were completely blacked out by stones. There were candles, a kitchen worktop, plates washed and left to dry, equipment stored in Tupperware boxes. There were camp beds too, and a stove and cut peats. There was wood and an axe. We felt very thankful. Shuna split some kindling, lit the fire, I grappled with the camp beds. The fire was lit – flames, hurrah. We took off our sodden trousers and socks, hung them on a string over the fire. There were even pegs, bright blue ones. I lit a candle that was half burned down in an empty wine bottle.

'There's no heat in the fire,' said Shuna, 'but maybe it'll come.' We got out our sleeping bags and made ready for the night. We ate a can of butter beans with sardines and Tabasco and drank the last of the whisky in our tea. We were happy.

We lay down expecting to sleep, knowing we needed to, knowing the next day would be long and hard. In the silence the house began to feel hostile. I looked up at the wood-lined ceiling in the firelight, it had cornicing and the thought *this was never a home* came to me. A damp cold gusted from the broken upstairs, down through the hole that the ladder disappeared into. I imagined other things coming down that ladder and turned towards the fire for warmth, but the peats burned a slow orange and put out no heat. My back was chilled and exposed to whatever was coming down from upstairs. Rolling back over, eyes wide and dry, I looked into the metal bulge of a 25kg gas bottle. I didn't pray, but I called on spirits, all those that had dwelt or passed through this place in the past centuries, millennia even, back to before the peat was deep. And other, more recent times when Cattle were milked up the river from here, and were walked north across the moor towards Uig. *Were they very small, or was the ground not so wet back then? Did they have a secret route, passed down through the generations? Had ponies ever been in this place?*

I'd assumed, because there were stalkers' paths on the map, and runrigs and houses, that there must have been ponies too. But maybe not, or perhaps they'd been brought in by boat, like the sheep we'd been told about. If all went wrong tomorrow, maybe we could take the ponies out by boat. I shuddered then, knowing I never wanted to see that grey boat again. It had grown monstrous in my mind, monstrous as the *each-uisge* (water horses) that lured women to their deaths. I was also aware of the irony that in this situation it was ourselves, and nobody else, who could be held responsible for any luring.

In the daylight Kinloch Rèasort had felt remote and isolated. In the peat-light, I felt the presence of past people. The last child born here was in 1907. Imagine going into labour out here, how terrifying it would have been if things went wrong. Remembering the three beads in the beehive south of here, I wanted to see my children. Badly. Fleas bit across my stomach, the camp beds were full of them. I scratched at my body, feeling the changes in texture where each stretch mark crossed my stomach. I scratched harder, tearing at my skin with peaty nails. I didn't sleep. There hadn't been any heat coming from the fire but when it finally died an even more intense cold descended.

I couldn't lie any longer so hopped to the window in my sleeping bag. An orange moon scudded behind frayed clouds. I had never felt so frightened in my life. There were occasional stars, bright specks between stealths of cloud. In his book *When Breath Becomes Air* Paul Kalanithi writes that 'the root of disaster means a star coming apart, and no image expresses better the look in a patient's eyes when hearing a neurosurgeon's diagnosis'. I looked at the moon and thought of Mum. I called on her quietly. Even though I'd promised I wouldn't, that I'd let her be, I called on her anyway, and acknowledged the fear she must have felt faced with death, such fear that even she, outspoken on all taboos, had chosen in the end not to speak of.

Lying on the canvas camp bed and looking out of the window, I got colder and colder. My mind started to disarticulate as the moon ratcheted across the window. On the border between Harris and Lewis, I was on a threshold between safe and unsafe, between the spirit world and the non-spirit world, between being stuck or unstuck. The Gaelic translation for the saying 'being stuck between a rock and a hard place' is *eadar dà theine Bealltainn*. Literally meaning between two Beltane fires. I had my fires, the gas and the peat, and now I was frozen. Would I be able to change? Could I be braver? Sheep bleated outside. I didn't feel it that night but in the months that followed I would see changes: I'd begin to say small 'no's to people and learn that the world didn't end; I'd let go of a friendship that had run its course. Yes, I'd learn to stop sitting on the fence, trying to cover all bases, to keep everybody happy. But that was all later. Now, in the watchers' house I was rigid and sleepless with fear. Haunted by the sight of Ross floundering in the bog and the call of the Greenshank. And all the while cold was burrowing into me. I must have fallen asleep, because I woke with my heart juddering.

The darkness was complete, the moon gone from the window. I sat up stiffly and hopped across again to press my nose flat against the pane. When I saw the moon a current jolted through me and, in that moment, I knew that everything was going to be all right. The feeling was as real and as fierce as the flea bites which would itch and bleed and scab for months to come.

DAY TWENTY
Loch Rèasort to Aird Asaig

'Peanut delight or cocoa orange?' asked Shuna. The oats were finished so breakfast was an energy bar. I was holding on to the moment in the night when I'd felt that wave of 'it will all be all right', but now, in the cold grey early morning, I just felt frightened.

'Cocoa orange.' I took a bite and forced it down. *Coffee might help, some caffeine-induced can-do.* All it did was twist my guts even tighter. With heavy arms I packed away the camp beds, stuffed my sleeping bag into its gossamer-thin cover and thought about leaving a thank-you note for the candles, now burned an inch lower, for the peats, for the beds. But that would be evidence we'd been there, uninvited, and right now I just wanted to get out of there, to forget about this place.

We laid our packed saddlebags outside. The boys were resting side by side in their favourite spot above the blackhouses on the other side of the bay. I looked up at the weighty skies, rain was on its way. If we needed to climb onto the tops it would be so much harder in poor visibility. We went back inside and put on our waterlogged boots. I thought about the scene in the film *Into the Wild* where McCandless, having gone out into the Alaskan wilderness to be alone, finally decides he wants to be back in human company, but then can't cross the rivers which are rising with meltwater. He dies.

Obviously, we're not in that predicament. Of course, we'll get out and no one's going to die. Anyway, as an absolutely last resort the ponies could get out on a boat, but my mind kept slipping. *Welcome to the last resort. You will never leave.*

I couldn't stop thinking about rising burns and mist coming down. About Ross half-lost to the peat yesterday, and how those two ponies were dependent on us to get them out of this mire we'd led them into. It felt like a completely different place to the one we'd walked into two days before, when we were drenched in evening sunshine and river water and sheer delight, and the Sea Eagle had fixed us with her bold eye. Now I was connected to a deep sense of sadness and fear. Was it all my own or was I also tuning in to the *cianalas*, the Gaelic word for what Alastair McIntosh describes as a 'soul-felt wearisomeness'? He goes on to say, 'that pretty much this whole western coastline of North Harris and South Lewis cries out, laconic in its emptiness'.

We closed the door, building the stones carefully back up in front of it.

'A spot of sunshine would be good,' said Shuna brightly. I nodded. 'What's that?' she said, pointing down to our right. A small boat was idling in towards the shore just to the north of us.

'It's not estate people again, is it?' I asked.

'I don't know,' said Shuna flatly.

My first thought was to hide. Then something firmed up inside me. 'Let's go and have a closer look, let's be grown-up about it.' We set off stumbling but together over the rocks.

'I think it might be walkers,' said Shuna. 'There's a woman and two men.' As we approached, a waterproof-clad couple, now standing on the shore, waved to us. I felt delight at seeing that gesture and those friendly, and thankfully unfamiliar, faces.

It turned out that the couple lived in Uig, up round the coast, and were being dropped off by their pal in the boat. They were planning to walk home around the coast to the north west, and were hoping to find a dozen beehive dwellings on the shore that were being eroded by the sea.

'They'll be gone soon,' said the woman, 'and we want to see them before they're washed away forever.'

We spilled out what had happened the day before: the bogs, the boat, the men. 'We didn't feel the love,' I said.

The man lifted an orange dry bag from the boat onto the rocks and put it down next to an empty rucksack, and other full dry bags. His face was serious. 'No,' he said. 'You wouldn't have been feeling the love. This is the playground of just a few, and those few don't want anyone out here. I'm local and I can tell you the clearances are very close here. That lot,' he tilted his head to the south west, 'they're obsessed with poachers.' As he spoke I watched his hands methodically pack the dry bags into his rucksack. The woman was doing the same. They were businesslike, and you could tell they were eager to be on their way as a thin slanting rain began to fall.

'Have you seen the forecast?' Shuna asked.

'It wasn't looking great,' said the woman. 'Heavy rain's coming in, but last year we waited for the good weather all summer and missed out, so this year we're just getting on with it.'

'We needed that,' said Shuna as we walked away. 'Some normal friendly people.' As we crossed the bay to the ponies the little boat buzzed away out of sight, a lone man at the helm. By the time we got to the field the walkers were well up the hillside across the loch, the woman's hi-vis waterproof pack cover was easy to spot. The man was ahead, harder to see against the darkening hillside. We would think of them on and off all day: wondering if they'd found their beehives yet;

voicing our gladness for them when the weather brightened; remembering them when the rain blew in cold and sharp. We were not alone.

At the far end of the sheep park I took the fishing net down from where I'd hung it across the gateway and, passing our camping spot, thanked the blackhouse for the comfortable camping spot, saw as if for the first time how the ground had grown up between the walls: four feet of earth and grass and moss since it had last been inhabited. We led the boys out of the sheep park, tied the gate shut behind them. My hands felt the roughness of the wiry yellow rope, *for the last time*, but part of me knew there was a chance we'd be back again that night.

We walked silently up the fishermen's path beside Abainn Thabhsaigh, funnelling our focus into each careful step. My legs felt weak with anxiety. Would Ross manage out in front today, or might he have lost his nerve after the horrors of yesterday? He walked out willingly, his steps steady and considered. My heart could have burst. Whether I was deserving of his trust or not, I had it. My legs started to move more fluently, my feet following the slender slots of deer.

Certainty is the enemy of poetry and love and faith.

I couldn't remember where I'd heard those words. We'd got to the bend in the river where we'd been advised to cut across the moor to the hillside, time to leave behind the deer slots and gravelly song of the river. The night before we'd picked out a line of rocks, but now we were full of doubt. I left Ross with Shuna and went ahead to scout once more. 'Okay, let's give this a go then,' I said when I returned. Ross and I went ahead, skirting the peat hags. We made it across to the first stony mound and chose a line to the next. It was going well when Shuna shouted out that Chief had fallen back into the underside of a peat bank and his hind legs were in deep. I felt sick. He couldn't get out the way he was facing. 'Shuna, if you can turn him to face downhill gravity might help him out.' It worked. The four of us stood side by side, taking a few moments to recover. Chief's peat-coated hocks a dark reminder of our predicament.

'We did it,' I said, when we finally reached the side of the hill. We gave each other a wan smile. We thought then that the hardest part was over, that we'd be able to follow the close contour lines of this hillside southwards towards the vehicle track that would take us out of here. Was it really just two days since we'd ridden up that track to the fishing bothy at Loch Boishimid? It felt like so much had happened since then that time had tangled up on itself.

Following the line of the hill as best we could we realised it wasn't going to be simple, the hillside was terraced with peat hags. 'We'll have to go higher,' I said tightly. Further up we found more of the same, stepping around sink after sink of peat. 'We're on a fucking hillside,' I said, in exasperation. 'Why is there so much peat up here?'

There were pools of quaking bog too. I didn't want to stop, worried that I'd never get going again. Keeping my legs moving forwards I didn't look back. Glad I wasn't behind, I would have hated watching Ross's legs sinking in time and again, and then having to follow. Each step was a step of faith. Finally, we reached a rocky shelf big enough for the four of us to take a breather. We were all blowing hard.

'This is a nightmare,' said Shuna. 'Any other way out, do you think? Could we get across there to the river?' She was pointing towards the hill we'd come down that first evening. I'd have done anything to be back there now, to scramble up that heathery nose, come across the dead deer remains again. Between us and the river was a mired mess of ground. Drumlins rose between endless glints of water and quivering patches of lurid green.

'I don't think there's any way we'll get across there,' I said. 'We'll have to stay on this side, and gain more height.' Mist was on the tops now. 'Maybe fifty yards or so higher things will improve, are you okay with that?' Shuna nodded.

I started to zigzag my way up, Ross following, uncomplaining despite the steep gradient. There was a sense of something spurring us onwards and upwards. Then, just as I thought we were getting onto firmer ground, Ross sank up to his belly. He lay there with a look of utter resignation on his face. He was in deep but there were rocks around us and I felt calm, this time I just knew he'd get out. He did, by turning to face downhill, and like Chief had done earlier, using gravity to ease his way out. Shuna afterwards said she got such a feeling in that moment from Ross, a feeling of deep tiredness, but also a feeling from him that we were all in this together. It was painfully clear to us now that the peat was pooled across this hillside, the landmarks were unreliable, and it would be a very long way back to the track at the speed we were going. We agreed that there was nothing else for it but to get right up onto the tops, that the side of the hill was just too unrelentingly unsafe. The day was getting colder, and as we started uphill again blinds of rain closed off the view of the glen. *Please, please, stay clear for us up there.*

From the top we could see over the other side and down towards the scalpel-blade glint of Loch Cheibhle. We stopped to catch our breath and the ponies snatched at thin bents of grass. It was a moonscape up there. Grey, cold bedrock crossed between massive balancing boulders. It was a landscape of leftovers and left behinds. I wished I still had my gloves, but they were lost somewhere on Uist. I pulled my buff up over my mouth, I was starting to shiver, my sweat cooling quickly. We carried on, staying as close to the top and the watershed as we could. Sometimes burns had cut into the rock making gullies that we had to follow down in order to find a safe crossing place, and we'd go all the way back up again as quickly as possible. Each time we lost height we were met with pools of peat. The ponies were magnificent. Up and down they went, their hooves clattering on the rocks. As we headed slowly towards the summit of Mullach na Redheachd a bloom of mist enfolded us, but cleared again. We came to a precipice where the hillside dropped away sharply and I shuddered imagining how much worse the conditions could have been for us up there that day.

We stepped back from the edge and debated our next move. It seemed we had a choice. We could try heading down the steep gully now visible to the north west which would take us down to Loch Uladail. The map showed a path picking up from there that would take us back to the car park. But between the head of the loch and the path we'd have to travel beneath the overhang, Stron Uladail, where the ground was littered with huge broken-away rocks. It was impossible to tell from where we were whether there would be a way through them. If there wasn't, we'd have to climb all the way up again. The other option was to keep going, and start heading slowly down to the south east. Either way was down, and both downs looked terrifying. I wondered what it would be like to stay the night up there. We were almost out of food but we had our sleeping bags and tent, although I didn't know how it would fare in this wind. A part of me that was expecting to see a search party out looking for us, surely someone would be worried about us by now. When I said that to Shuna she laughed. 'Who do you think will be worried? They'll just be thinking we're out of phone signal and having a great time.'

Wondering which would be the best route down, listening for an answer in the mist, no answer came, and we went around in circles discussing the possible advantages and disadvantages of each route. In the end we opted for the better known option, and began to head slantwise down across the hillside towards Loch Bhoishimid and the wooden bothy we'd had our coffee at three days earlier. We didn't stop for another two hours, not allowing our momentum and nerve to flag, until we reached the track eight hours after we'd left the bothy that morning. Eight hours to travel just a few kilometres! But we'd made it back to hard ground. We cried. Of course, we cried. And then we walked those delicious last miles on hard track, thinking our own thoughts, stepping out our own fears, letting the spaces between us widen because, mercifully, it was safe to do so.

I hadn't thought about Mum all that day, being too busy working with my wits, staying safe, surviving. I had been fully in my body, in my animal being, no space for guilt or reminiscence. That long list of regrets that had been haunting me for years was silent, the one that ran on and on: *I wish I'd gone in for cups of tea, I wish I'd taken her to eat mussels on the pier in Oban that sunny April day, I wish I'd gone in to talk to the surgeon with her, I wish I wish I wish I'd done this, and not that, and definitely not that, and if only things could have been different between us while she was alive.* All those regrets that made me fold over in pain. The ones I would never speak out loud, the ones I turned over and over and over in my mind. That day coming out of Kinloch Rèasort my head emptied into the banks of the burns, between peat hags, across the stony surface of the hilltops. That would have been the place to have left a bead for her, on that lunar ridge, but I hadn't. Instead I'd left a part of Beady, a part of myself, that I no longer needed. There is a word, *puhpowee*, from the Potawatomi Nation, which describes the force that causes mushrooms to push up and appear overnight. I felt a new me had emerged after my night in the bothy. I'd left behind that old skin quilted with guilt. I felt raw, taken to the bone, but also excitedly ready for something different.

I waited by the padlocked gate with Ross and Chief while Shuna hitched a lift with some birders to Aird Asaig. It would be an hour or so before she returned with the pickup. I listened to the sea slap the shore and watched the boys graze. Late sun broke through the showers. I went to the saddlebags looking for the honey, remembering something I'd read in *Poacher's Pilgrimage*, that 'the right time to feed the faeries (...) is when the rain is still raining, and the sun is beginning to shine'. I squeezed drops onto the rocks, amongst the heather and hedges. *For the Faeries. Let Mum, the woman who taught me to believe in Faeries, just be a part of me now. Let that be enough. Let it be enough that this evening I am just leaving honey for the Faeries, and watching two brilliant Ponies graze in the rain.*

DAY TWENTY-ONE
Aird Asaig to Callanish

It was wonderful to wake in a comfy bed. I looked at my phone screen, 8.30am. My nails were still black with peat despite the bath I'd had the night before. Shuna had been right and there were no messages on my phone when we got back into signal, not even a missed call. Katie-Anne, Corina and Lauren had welcomed us back into their home in Tarbert at short notice. I looked at the two inches of sky between the curtains, the zinc cloud of yesterday was gone. It was all blue. We wouldn't be riding into Callanish as we'd planned, or north to the Butt of Ness, not on this trip anyway. Today was our last full day in the Outer Hebrides, but I didn't feel a trace of disappointment, just deep relief and gratitude. This journey had been richer in experience and meaning, both physical and emotional, than I could have ever imagined. Here we were back in Tarbert amongst some of the kindest people I'd ever met, and most importantly of all Ross and Chief were safe and sound a few miles away in Kenny's field at Aird Asaig.

Months later we'd go to a talk in Oban Library that Alastair McIntosh was giving. During the tea break we shared a little of our story with him, and I gave him a tattered copy of *Poacher's Pilgrimage* to sign. Handing it back he'd fixed me with a steady eye. His writing was wiry, slanted, like windblown Marram

Grass: *For Leonie, To take a rucksack was one thing, but a pony – that blows my mind. Very best wishes, Alastair McIntosh.*

For the second time we said our goodbyes to Katie Ann and her girls. We stopped at the Harris Gin Distillery where Kenny worked as a Manager. On the wall was a large photograph of him and Bella. Kenny was leaning against a Stoneleigh Grey Massey Ferguson, smiling across at his daughter who was balancing on the tyres and smiling back at him, her fingers interlaced, a mirror image of her father's. It was a picture of mutual devotion. We bought bottles of gin to take home, the colour of the sea at Eoligarry. Barra felt like a very long time ago now. Back at Aird Asaig the loch was a shade deeper than the azure sky. Starlings chattered on telegraph wires and hills lifted sheer and clear ahead of us. Below, at the head of the loch, the chimney of the Whale Station was a strike of brick-red.

'My granny used to talk about the smell,' said the lady in the petrol station, wrinkling up her nose, when we asked. But today the air was fresh and pristine. The ponies' backs shone in the sunshine, but below their bellies, on their knees and fetlocks and threaded through their tails, were the gluey shadows of peat.

The roads were quiet. The ponies had stepped unhesitatingly into the horsebox, were now munching on full nets of haylage as we drove along the A859 towards Stornoway. The road was smooth and easy. Water Lilies were beginning to bloom on the hill lochs. We drove through the strung-out village of Ballalan. 'Look,' said Shuna, nodding at a man in front of his bungalow. 'You don't see that very often.' The man was cutting his lawn with a scythe. We passed several bungalows with antlers above the garage.

That autumn I'd meet a man who used to work for Amhuinnsuibhe estate and was familiar with the house we'd stayed in at Kinloch Rèasort. He talked about walking in there with his dog on a Friday night for a drink with 'the watchers' and described the route over from Hamnavay, hard-going and pathless, between deep hill lochs full of Arctic Char. How he'd spot the occasional triple-fleeced tup. 'You could see the pixies and faeries in their eyes.'

He talked of the multi-winter Salmon running up the rivers, the world-renowned Sea Trout, how the locals hated to be told they couldn't fish in places they'd been fishing since they were kids. How they hated the English, how *he* was all right because he was half Welsh. It wasn't just the fish people were poaching. He spoke of the village of Balallan, 'where each house has a quad shelter and antlers on the wall. Poachers,' he said, 'they do it just for devilment, they don't need the money. The estate tried to prosecute them, but it didn't go down very well.' He told me how he and his colleagues used to shoot Deer for the estate on that ground by the disappeared postal track to Morscaig.

'It would be emotional,' he said, 'getting them out, but I'd go back there in a heartbeat.'

Shuna and I drove on to Stornoway and then took the Pentland Road west. This route was built in the 1890s, originally designed for horse-drawn vehicles. It was gently graded and passed through moorland dotted with shielings. Most were ruins now, they'd originally been built of stone, and peat-turf roofs with a hole in the centre to let out smoke from the central hearth. There were also more modern ones made of tin although some were already falling down: a slow collapse of roof, the flake and peel of paint and rust. Others had been done up. Glints of galvanised steel roof, a newly painted red door. It was comforting to be in the pickup, travelling through the gently undulating moors that spread out in all directions. Yesterday's hills were a mere bruise on the south horizon, wind turbines flashed cumulus-white between there and here. A Curlew flew across the rough grasses, and an old lady wearing a pink skirt, working alone at the peats, looked up as we passed and smiled. What a picture, just her and the Curlew, out in all of that.

Emily, who'd been following our journey on Facebook, had given us a contact for a field in Callanish. We met Sheena in the car park at the Callanish Visitor Centre. Her husband Cudaig, she explained, was in the Coastguard with Emily. We followed her car half a mile to their croft. 'This is ideal,' we said as Sheena showed us the field, pointing out where the water was. Chief and Ross explored for a while, then put their heads down to graze and we went off to put up the tent. Later, riding bareback, we set off down the road. The sound of hoof-horn on hard tarmac was bliss.

Within minutes the standing stones of Callanish I came into sight and we had the place entirely to ourselves. We rode the ponies through a gate and wandered in silence amongst those megaliths of Lewisian gneiss. Even sitting on the ponies we were dwarfed by the stones. Ross and Chief reached out and touched them with their noses, these stones that had been there for millennia. A German couple arrived, smiling, huge camera lenses resting in the crooks of their arms like babies. I asked them if they'd take a photo of us and handed them my phone. I have the picture now, us amongst those stones that reached into a sky awash with clouds – stones and clouds and ponies, and our wide wind-chapped smiles. We continued down the road and along a track towards Callanish II. A stile straddled the stock fence, there was no way through for the boys so we left them tied. Over their backs we could make out Callanish I, a host of stones on the horizon.

Callanish II and III were altogether wilder places. There was no mowed grass here and I felt at home with the mellow smell of cow dung. Even this late in the evening Skylarks were singing. Every once in a while, a vehicle would judder across the cattle grid on the main road. Snipe drummed against the last of the day. I sat down with my back against a sloping stone. Here most of the stones stood at rakish angles, the Cattle and Sheep had made hollows in the ground where they sheltered and rubbed against them. On some stones tufts of cattle hair clung to the Lichen, on others the marbled rock had been polished smooth. 'The Cattle must love it here,' I said. Later, over a cup of tea and a plate of delicious drop scones, Sheena, who was the Common Grazings Clerk, told us that Historic Scotland had sent her a letter inviting her to come and look at the damage the beasts were doing. 'What did you say to them?' I asked. 'Ach, I let the letter lie,' she answered, her eyes shining.

'I think we deserve a toast,' said Shuna, walking over from the stone she'd been leaning against and passing me the hip flask.

'To these stones, to us, to Skylarks, to Chief and Ross,' she said. I took a long sip of Oban 14 year old – *light on the peat, notes of cut hay, tarry ropes and the sea.*

'Here's to Mum, who loved the smell of hot tar. To Mum, who loved so much.'

We walked the ponies slowly back towards Callanish I. We couldn't resist a last daunder amongst the stones. I put my hand on rock that had been crushed and melted and folded for over 3,000 million years, rock that was embedded with crystals of feldspar, white quartz, hornblende, rock that had been shaped and raised by a people five thousand years ago. To the east of us a soft cottony moon, one day off full, was surfacing in the sky.

'Why don't we come back at sunrise?' said Shuna. 'Yes!' I said. *Perfect. I'd leave beads here for Mum as the sun rose, I'd leave the last of the beads.* I tilted my face up, and in the sweep of sky overhead found two Swarovski-sharp stars. Even the way I saw the stars was informed by Mum, watching her working with all those crystals, seeing her thread them, turning them bead by bead into works of art. My appreciation of being here now, of this place, of this everything, was intensified because she'd embedded in me a love of antiquity, of discovery, of Scotland, of Horses.

DAY TWENTY-TWO

Sunrise at Callanish

The alarm went off at 3.30am. I was instantly awake, we had less than an hour to pack the tent, load Chief and Ross and drive along to Callanish I before sunrise at 4.24am. There was a strong tangerine glow on the horizon and my heart raced with a childlike excitement. We made it just in time and were standing by the stone-drawn cruciform as the sun rose. I spun round slowly, taking it all in, our shadows going on forever, the stones turning an earthy pink. The sky folded into mauves and azures, a breath of cloud turned scarlet in a single second. Then the whole of the sun was visible between the stones, their shadows reaching across the turf. I walked down the longest shadow to a large flat rock, knelt and emptied the bead purse. There were four left: an unpolished lapis bead; a handmade glass bead – cobalt blue and tubular; a branch of red coral; an off-round seed pearl. It was perfect, to leave the last of beads here, at Callanish, as the sun climbed.

I stood up and walked away from the beads towards a solitary standing stone. Behind it were the silver reaches of Loch Ceann Hùlabhaig, in the far distance I could see those dark hills we had been in only two days before. The whole of my shadow fitted on the stone. The rock was ridged like an oyster shell and the striations ran through me. That was me. Beady. Me. Leonie. Mum had named me after a French writer. 'Léonie,' she'd say with her perfect French accent. I'd always shied away from my name, it was somehow too big, too brave, too lion-like for me. Maybe now it was time to step into it, my name given to me by a beautiful young woman some forty-five years ago who believed in Faeries, in her children, and that the world was their oyster.

'Look, a Short Eared Owl,' I said. We were driving slowly across the moorland towards Stornoway, in good time to catch the 7am ferry to Ullapool. The bird glided for long soft seconds before disappearing over a knoll.

'That might be the last one we see for a while,' I added.

'I can't wait to come back,' said Shuna. From the tone of her voice I knew we shared the same yearning.

I looked in the side mirror, saw Ross's ears, forelock, one calm eye, and in that moment felt radiant and full of love: love for Ross, for Shuna, for Chief; love for these islands, their people and wildlife and landscapes; love for all and everyone I was travelling home to. And there was something else: this journey had helped me find a way to let go of the guilt and pain which had been silting inside me for so many years. In its place acceptance, for Mum, for myself, for the two of us, had flowed in a little each day. I opened the window and reached both hands out, letting the cold air burn through my fingers, light rising, rising on that clear June morning.

I'm ready to stop chasing the idea of a better relationship. I'm ready to stop hounding the 'what ifs', and for the 'what ifs' to stop hounding me. It was what it was, Mum. Deeply flawed. Real. Human. Difficult. You were impossible. I was impossible. And all the same we loved each other. It was far from perfect. But it's enough to know that I loved you, that I love you now, that I feel you in me when I see a Spider threading her silk web, a Bat feeding in the evening air, each time I smell the velvet muzzle of a Horse. I'll be travelling paths you opened to me for the rest of my life, travelling them with lion-hearted love.

Mum and Me, Anglesey, 1974